Operation
White Lion

Operation White Lion

Chris McBride

St. Martin's Press
New York

Library of Congress Cataloging in Publication Data

McBride, Chris, 1941-
    Operation white lion.

    Sequel To: The white lions of Timbavati.
    1. Lions.   2. Mammals—South Africa—Timbavati Game
Reserve.   3. Timbavati Game Reserve (South Africa)
I. Title.
QL737.C23M29   599.74′428   81-8839
ISBN 0-312-58680-9   AACR2

10 9 8 7 6 5 4 3 2 1
First Edition

To two of the three women I love:
my mother and my daughter.

CONTENTS

Illustrations between pages 32 and 33, 64 and 65, 112 and 113, 144 and 145

ACKNOWLEDGEMENTS

Some people helped selflessly; others merely helped. I thank them all.

Jack Mathebula	John Dunning
Glenn Cowley	Petri Viljoen
Keith Joubert	Trygve Cooper
Mandaban Hlongo	Sheri Safran
Cyril McBride	Bruce Blair Crawford
Tabby	Nick Hancock
Charlotte	

Tony Gray did invaluable work sifting through tape transcripts to produce a book; Marjorie Villiers and Ernestine Novak carried on the good work. Professor Archie S. Mossman, of Humboldt State University, California, was always there with the kind of encouragement and constructive criticism that I needed.

Savuti, Botswana, 1980

Photographs taken by Peter Dixon: No. 1; Petri Viljoen: Nos 9a, 29a, 31a, 31b, 31c.

All other photographs by Chris McBride.

PUBLISHER'S NOTE

These introductory notes may be useful for those readers of *Operation White Lion* who are not familiar with the author's earlier book, *The White Lions of Timbavati*.

Chris McBride, a South African, now resident in Botswana, decided to study a pride of lions in depth while working for a Master's Degree in Wildlife Management. His choice fell on one which occupied the Machaton range in the private Nature Reserve at Timbavati. He chose to observe the Machaton lions on the assumption that they would be a representative pride. In the event this proved far from true for two cubs, white as polar bears, were born to one of the lionesses. They were genuine white – not albinos. Though there were old legends about white lions in Africa, none had ever been seen.

The Machaton pride consisted of Achilles and Agamemnon, two magnificent male lions, who ruled over six lionesses: Golden, Dimples, Scarleg, Greta, Lona and Tabby, the smallest of them.

Golden was known to have given birth to three males usually called the three Musketeers and one female, Suzie Wong. These young lions were now of an age equivalent to teenagers in human beings.

Tabby had given birth to the two white cubs, Temba, a male and Tombi, a female, and also to Vela, a tawny brother. They were probably fathered by Agamemnon and were much younger than Golden's brood.

The Machaton pride had neighbours: the Velvet Paws pride, and the Sohebele lions who were known to be much fiercer than the other two groups.

Operation White Lion begins when, on his return from Europe, Chris McBride is faced with an alarming development among the Machaton lions which may well mean death to the white cubs.

xiii

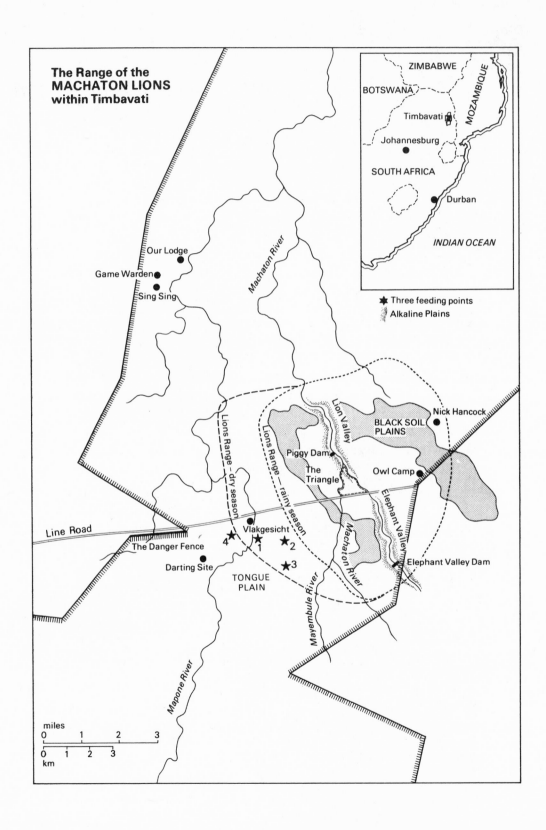

The Range of the MACHATON LIONS within Timbavati

ZIMBABWE

BOTSWANA

MOZAMBIQUE

Timbavati

Johannesburg

SOUTH AFRICA

Durban

INDIAN OCEAN

★ Three feeding points

Alkaline Plains

Our Lodge

Game Warden

Sing Sing

Machaton River

Lion Valley

Nick Hancock

BLACK SOIL PLAINS

Piggy Dam

The Triangle

Owl Camp

Lions Range — dry season

Lions Range — rainy season

Elephant Valley

Machaton River

Line Road

Vlakgesicht

★4 ★1 ★2

★3

The Danger Fence

Darting Site

Elephant Valley Dam

TONGUE PLAIN

Mavembule River

Mapone River

miles
0   1   2   3

0   1   2   3
km

CHAPTER 1

Where is Agamemnon?

'I think something terrible has happened to Agamemnon: I don't believe we shall ever see him again.' These words were spoken by my Zulu friend and assistant, Jack Mathebula, while we were eating our Christmas dinner – in a thatched *rondavel* in Timbavati, North Eastern Transvaal, where I was managing a private game lodge. Now, seven thousand miles away, as I drove to London Airport at the end of a visit to my publishers, the words echoed insistently in my mind. I was returning to Timbavati; when I reached home would there be news of the magnificent Agamemnon? If not, my first task would be to search for him.

I would not have been so worried by Jack's remark but for the fact that he has an uncanny instinct about such things. Whenever in the past we have lost track of our pride of lions, I have tried to find them by spooring, or by listening at night to their roars and then taking a compass bearing; but Jack just seemed to know where they were. He had been brought up in the bush and had never been to school, so he had not developed a cause-and-effect mind. I believe that reasoning interferes with the brain's ability to function instinctively, as it does for some animals and with some early races such as the bushmen of West Africa.

The last time I had seen Agamemnon and Achilles, the other great lion of the Machaton pride, they had been together, as they usually were. They had always been very close and, from my observation, I concluded that they were brothers, possibly twins. I thought that at one time they had been nomads together and that at some stage, before I started to study the Machaton pride in depth for my degree in Wildlife Management, these lions had taken over the Machaton range and its six lionesses: Tabby, the mother of the white lions, Temba and Tombi, Golden, Scarleg, Dimples, Greta and Lona.

They had been well when I had seen them last, two months earlier. Their absence had not disturbed me greatly because they had a habit of wandering off on their own, sometimes for days on end, marking out their territory and roaring at various points along the fringe of the range to discourage any nomad from an adjoining pride who might think of invading their kingdom. While I was working on my book, *The White Lions of Timbavati*, the pride had divided itself into two sub-groups, one consisting of Tabby and her three cubs, the two whites and their tawny brother plus Dimples, Tabby's great friend, who was helping her to feed and look after the cubs. The other sub-group consisted of the three fully grown lionesses with ten young cubs including a third white lioness, Phuma, and a 'teenage' lioness, Suzie Wong, who, like Dimples, helped the three lionesses to look after their cubs. Suzie Wong had two teenage brothers, called the Musketeers (there had been three, but I had been obliged to shoot one when he charged me). A nomad lion, thrown out by one of the neighbouring prides, had now joined the Machaton pride to fill the gap created by the death of the third Musketeer.

We called the newcomer the Interloper. He was a fine young lion, slightly older than the Musketeers. These three male lions commuted regularly between Tabby's group and the main sub-group and so, up to the time I had last seen them, had Agamemnon and Achilles. This was a normal, stable social system, very common among lion prides. The lionesses of the main sub-group refused to let Tabby's cubs come anywhere near their much younger offspring, partly because four adult lionesses and ten cubs take a lot of feeding so there might not be enough to go round, and partly because Temba, Tombi and Vela were now big enough to injure the smaller cubs if they were on a kill.

Earlier, Tabby had rigorously excluded Suzie Wong and the

Musketeers from her group for the same reason, but now she reckoned that her cubs were old enough to look after themselves. This is the system by which lions have ruled for millions of years and the fact that lions still survive in the wild is proof that it works.

The stability of the whole system, however, depends on strict government from above. If the pride males should be defeated and thrown out by males from an adjoining pride, or by marauding nomad lions, anything could happen. It has been observed that a marked increase in cub mortality usually follows such a change in regime and sometimes the lionesses do not begin to breed again for several months. That is why Jack's premonition that something had happened to Agamemnon worried me so much.

In the plane I went on thinking about the Machaton pride. I had picked them purely by chance as the basis of a thesis I had planned to write on one pride of lions, studying them in depth from a caged jeep. The cage was to keep out the lions, though no doubt if they had been determined to get in, they would have done so. However, it gave me a sense of security and enabled me to make my observations with a moderately tranquil mind. In the event, the lions completely ignored me and behaved as though the jeep were not there.

When I chose the Machaton pride I was staying with my wife Charlotte and daughter Tabitha at my father's camp, Vlakgesicht, on a private nature reserve. A large segment of the Machaton lions' range ran through my father's land. That this pride happened to give birth to the world's first known true white lions (not albinos, but genuine white lions with tawny eyes and fur as white as a polar bear's) was not relevant to my thesis. Indeed it was rather an embarrassment because I had chosen the Machaton as a *typical* pride.

If Jack were right, and we were not going to see Agamemnon again, what could have happened to him? He had been very fit when I last saw him, and was still in his prime, one of the finest lions I have ever seen. There was no way in which he could have been pulled down by a pack of marauding hyenas, the commonest fate of old and ailing lions. It was possible he might have wandered into the adjoining Kruger National Park. A small segment of the Machaton range lies within the Kruger and lions can wriggle under the fence. I had been alarmed by rumours of a lion-culling operation in this area.

The most likely explanation for Agamemnon's disappearance was that he had wandered too deep into the Kruger and been shot. If that had happened I could perhaps confirm it by making discreet enquiries to discover whether anybody remembered anything about the death of a big, black-maned lion with a damaged eye.

If, on the other hand, he had somehow been injured and brought down by predators, there would be no way in which we could ever know for certain what had happened. If he had been killed it might have happened anywhere within an area of thirty square miles and, within twenty-four hours, all trace of him would have disappeared. Hyenas, vultures and jackals would have demolished the flesh; hyenas would also have crushed the bones and scattered them far and wide as well as eating the skin. The killers of the wild, unlike their human counterparts, leave little evidence behind to tell the tale.

I now remembered something that had happened just before I left for London. I was driving round the range of an adjoining pride – one we knew as the Velvet Paws – and I was surprised to find Achilles lurking behind a *kopje* flirting with one of their lionesses.

I could see what he was after from his own point of view, for at that time all the Machaton lionesses were preoccupied with their cubs and not available for mating, so what was more natural than that Achilles should slip next door to fulfil his needs? On the other hand, the whole cohesion of a pride system depends on the dominance of the pride male, or males, and it was unlikely that the Velvet Paws male would have allowed Achilles to take such an audacious liberty without a struggle. If such a struggle had taken place, obviously Achilles had been the victor. Possibly he had ousted the Velvet Paws male and himself taken over the pride.

If this were so and if Agamemnon had disappeared, this left the Machaton pride in a very vulnerable position with only the two teenage Musketeers and the Interloper to protect them, and the Interloper had not, from my observation, been accepted as a fully grown lion by the Machaton lionesses. When I had last seen them they were making submissive gestures to Tabby and the other pride lionesses.

When I reached the Jan Smuts airfield I rang Charlotte and she told me that the rains had suddenly started in real earnest. One of the bridges I would have to cross had been inundated to a depth of six feet so she thought I would have to take a roundabout route to reach home.

The weather had been very peculiar that year; normally the rains start around the beginning of November, but in 1976 they had not begun till 10 December, and even then only a few inches of rain had fallen. From then on until February there had been a virtual drought, even though this is as a rule the wettest part of the year. The result had been that the game had concentrated round the water holes and, since lions are to be found wherever their prey are, in these circumstances they are usually easy to discover.

This made the fact that Agamemnon had not been seen all the more significant. Another curious feature was that though it is the almost invariable rule among lion prides that as soon as the young sub-adult males reach the age of two and a half or three years and begin to represent a sexual challenge to the pride males, they are chased away to become nomads until such time as they can find a pride of their own to take over. Now since I had seen the Musketeers and the Interloper with the Machaton pride up to the time of my departure this, too, might point to the fact that Achilles and Agamemnon were no longer in control.

I could not wait to take the local plane back to Phalaborwa and find out what had been happening. Phalaborwa, the airport nearest to our camp, is a strip of grass with a terminal building about the size of a public lavatory. As soon as the plane landed I dashed into the pick-up truck and set off like a bat out of hell for the Reserve. Luckily the river had subsided by then and I was able to cross it.

As I drove into the compound I was met by Charlotte with our new son Robert, and Tabitha, whom we usually call Tabs. Delighted as we were to be together again, the occasion was marred by the fact that since I had left there had been no sign of Tabby and her white cubs, and there had been no sign of Agamemnon or even of Achilles. Petri Viljoen, an official of the Division of Nature and Conservation, was visiting when I arrived. He confirmed that there had been a fairly extensive lion-culling operation in the Kruger, so that it was possible that Agamemnon had met his end there. He promised to try to find out whether a lion answering to Agamemnon's description had been among those shot. He was not very hopeful of getting an answer, but I felt that if Agamemnon was dead it did not matter very much how he had died.

I now went through my records. I had last seen Tabby and the white cubs on Christmas Day, and that was two months earlier. The last time I had seen Phuma, the third white, and her sub-group was on 11 January. In the bush, although nothing changes fundamentally in millions of years, a lot can happen in a couple of days. My first task would be to try to find the lions again, but my heart was heavy. I did not really believe that, deprived of the protection of Agamemnon and Achilles, the pride could have survived.

CHAPTER 2

A Problem Solved

Before I went out to look for the lions I wanted to hear what had happened to Charlotte during my absence. She had had an eventful time.

A few days after I left, the Sohebele lions, a very fierce pride, had made a kill just outside our fence. Charlotte said they had made 'quite a lot of noise', but she was not particularly worried because she had a rifle between the sheets with her. As for Tabs, she slept through it all. In the morning they went out to investigate, and found the remains of a cheetah and a few scattered bones of an impala. They assumed that the cheetah had killed the impala and was in the process of dining off it when the lions had arrived, killed the cheetah and proceeded to devour both him and what was left of the impala. All that remained of the cheetah were the paws and the skull, which Charlotte had kept for me. From the state of the fur I guessed that the cheetah had been dying anyway, for it was very pale and a lot of its hair had fallen off.

Normally lions do not kill cheetahs. They can't. They are not nearly fast enough. I mention this because if word got round that the Sohebele lions had killed a cheetah outside our camp this would give some of the landowners the excuse they need to start shooting lions on the grounds that cheetah are much rarer animals than lions, and if they kill the lions this will be the best way to increase the number of cheetah. This may sound good reasoning, but in fact it is nonsense and is based on a common fallacy, that of drawing conclusions from an isolated instance, or at any rate from an inadequate number of samples. It is true that lion will eat cheetah – they will eat anything that comes their way – but a healthy cheetah can outrun any lion. In this instance it was relevant that I had, some weeks earlier, seen and photographed an ailing cheetah with extremely weak hind legs not far from the camp, so this was probably the one the lions got. Statistically, lions account for less than one per cent of the cheetah death rate, so shooting lions would have no perceptible effect on the cheetah population.

Charlotte went on with her story, and I was not pleased, but also not surprised, to learn that while I had been in England not only did she go walking alone in the veldt, which is potentially dangerous, but that she actually took Tabs and little Robert with her. They had gone into the bush to shoot a francolin, an African species of pheasant; she had walked in front with a gun followed by Tabs carrying Robert in her arms. I pointed out that this seemed a little foolhardy. Charlotte's reply was 'But what could I do? I needed a francolin for the pot!' This was characteristic, for she thinks nothing of sleeping out in the bush in the back of a pick-up truck, and neither does Tabs. She told me that a few days later she had been visiting Tryg Cooper, the Game Warden, and on her way noticed a lot of elephant spoor on the dirt road that ran past the Coopers' house, and on to Sohebele, the only other game lodge in Timbavati. Charlotte asked the Coopers if they had seen any elephant, and Trish, Tryg's wife, said there had been an elephant standing right outside their bedroom window all night staring at them. Far from being frightened, Trish, who resembles Charlotte in her casual attitude to danger, had found this highly amusing.

Tabs also had a story to tell. One night a snake came into the camp and her mother killed it. Not that Charlotte thought the incident worth mentioning to me; she was far more interested in the fact that one evening when she and Tabs were sitting on the verandah they had heard a vervet monkey making a great fuss. Obviously he had been frightened by something so they ran out to discover the cause and saw, right in front of the camp, the first wild dogs they had ever seen in Timbavati.

Wild dogs have a curiously graceful, loping gait, heads held high. I think this distinctive gait may have been developed because they have to cover enormous distances. They are hardly ever seen in Timbavati – indeed I had never seen any up to now though later I observed packs of them on several occasions. They run down their prey sometimes working in relays. When the dog in front starts to get tired he falls back and lets the others take over the running. They have a very nasty reputation, and are shot on sight by many hunters. This is because they literally tear their prey apart while it is still running, and go on until it drops from loss of blood. Not pleasant, but this is the wild, and these are wild animals. Concepts such as sportsmanship or chivalry did not arise until mankind was fairly highly developed, though there are vague precursors of such sentiments, for example in the primates. Male baboons have been known quite deliberately to risk and sometimes lose their lives in what appears to be a defence of the remainder of their troop from attack by a leopard.

As soon as I had recovered from jet lag my first job was to acquire a new diesel Land Rover. I had a Volkswagen Combi, but it was out of order. This is the effect I seem to have on all mechanical contrivances, so now it would have to be towed into the nearest town, Hoedspruit, for repairs. In any case I needed a vehicle with a four-wheel drive for without one it was impossible to negotiate the bush during the rainy season.

Once I had a Land Rover things were a lot easier and I was able to begin a systematic search for the lions. On my first day out I saw only a leopard. There are in fact plenty around – perhaps a hundred – but they are very rarely to be seen, indeed in the years I have spent tramping through the bush and driving all over Timbavati in a jeep, I have only seen leopards on five occasions. They are quite unlike lions who sleep most of the time. In fact you could often go right up to a lion and almost stumble over him before he would wake up and bother to move off. Leopards, on the other hand, are always alert. They hunt by night and we often hear them coughing or on a kill, but on the rare occasions when you see them during the day time they are equally wide awake.

On this, my first search since my holiday, I saw some vultures circling a spot not far off the track. This could have meant a lion kill, but they flew away on the approach of the Land Rover, and since there was a strong wind blowing, the kill could have been anywhere within a radius of a quarter of a mile from the spot over which they were circling. To look for them would have been a tedious and probably fruitless exercise.

I therefore drove on to Lion Valley, one of the big alkaline areas along the Machaton near Piggy Dam, a place where lions used to enjoy resting in the hot, dry weather. However, it was now wet and windy, so I did not have any great hopes of finding them there; it was much more likely that they were lurking in the riverine bush. I found the valley crowded with wildlife: fifty zebra, about fifteen giraffe and a lone wildebeest. This was a sure indication that there were no lions in the vicinity, for had there been there would not have been another animal in sight.

As I drove back to camp I passed through an area that had recently been burned by the Game Warden. Burning is a subject that arouses much controversy, but it is standard practice in wildlife management for it is essential to burn the heavy vegetation and allow the young, fresh grass to grow – a form of enforced rotational grazing, in effect. Moreover, it has a precedent, for, from prehistoric times, towards the end of the dry season electric storms have always caused immense bush fires which perform precisely this task. The only difference today is that, because the land is fenced in, wildlife cannot migrate freely so it is necessary to build fire-breaks (wide, graded paths across which the fire cannot jump) to prevent the planned fire from spreading. When the Game Warden began his 1976 burning programme, the area scheduled for the 'hot' zone included the whole of the Machaton range and by the end of October two-thirds of it had been burned. The schedule required that the remaining third should be burned a week later.

The time to burn is a difficult decision. Ideally the burning should take place before the first rains; if you burn at this time you destroy all the old grass without inhibiting the growth of the new grass. Unfortunately, it is of course impossible to tell for certain

24

when the rains will come. In this case, so great was the Warden's concern for the white lions that before the remaining third was due to be burned he and I drove round the area already dealt with to see whether the new grass had yet started to grow and whether consequently the game had returned. Normally, after a hot burn the area presents a scene of utter desolation for a week or so, then the rains come and within a few days the first shoots of fresh new grass appear and the game comes flocking back because they find this new grass very delectable. However, now when we toured the range we found that since the rains had not yet started properly the area was still completely black, with no sign of new growth. So, purely for the sake of the white lions, Tryg Cooper interrupted his programme and left the remaining third unburned. This third was in my father's farm, Vlakgesicht – Vlak for short – where the lions stayed until about three weeks later when we had some rain and the burned area began to sprout. Then the game returned and the lions began to use the whole range again. Unfortunately, by this time, the old grass round Vlak was too wet to burn so this part of Tryg's scheme had to be abandoned. When you consider that the fire-breaks around each block have to be freshly graded each year, and that this operation costs over £4000, if you don't burn a block you had planned to burn, it means wasting a great deal of money. However, Tryg was not prepared to proceed with the burning if there were any possibility that it might drive the white lions off their range in search of food and into areas where they could be in danger from other prides, or from the guns of farmers.

The following day some guests arrived, and I was kept busy looking after them. During their three-day visit we covered sixty-eight miles but the only lions' spoor we saw was that of Phuma's group. From the direction in which the spoor was leading it looked as though they were still living on Vlak. During one of these drives I saw my first wild dogs, probably the same pack that Charlotte had seen while I was in London. We were driving through the bush one morning when we observed vultures going down to what must have been a kill. I drove towards them and saw eight giraffes standing in a row looking intently at one spot. When we got closer we saw that they were looking at eight wild dogs resting on the alkaline plain after feeding on a young wildebeest they had killed. They were evidently as much of a novelty to the giraffes as they were to me.

From now on I was out nearly every day looking for the lions. On one occasion in March I came across the spoor of a sub-group and it seemed to me that they were the Velvet Paws pride. This was what I would have expected if Agamemnon were dead and Achilles had deserted the pride. They were resting on Lion Plain, which is only about a mile and a half from Piggy Dam, and right in the heart of the Machaton pride's range. This was the first time I had seen strange lions in their territory. Perhaps it was because Achilles was with them and this offered immunity to the lionesses, for normally they would have been seen off the premises.

This incident, and the fact that the Musketeers and the Interloper had not yet been thrown out of the pride, indicated to me that the firm regime had now definitely collapsed. Then I remembered that about two months earlier Jack Mathebula had mentioned that he had seen three fully grown nomad lions about half a mile from the fringe of the Machaton range. At the time this had not disturbed me, but now, combined with the other strange happenings, I felt uneasy. Perhaps these nomads had taken over all or some of the Machaton pride lionesses, and if that were so, what would happen to the cubs? There might be a few sharp battles, if not an all-out war, with consequent peril to them.

I went to bed that night in a very disturbed state of mind – the more I thought about the situation, the more frightening the prospect seemed to be. It was on Friday 25 March that I found the big sub-group again, and as I suspected, there had been casualties. Luckily, Phuma was not among them, but three of the cubs were missing. The four lionesses and the two Musketeers were there. I was overjoyed to see them again; it was like meeting old friends after a long separation.

They were lying in a spot where I had so often seen them, just off one of their regular routes on the far side of the river from Lion Valley.

None of the lions, except the Musketeers, exhibited the slightest interest in the Land Rover. They were all flat out, tails swishing slowly, probably to keep off the flies. Some of them were lying on their backs with their paws in the air, the very picture of peace and lazy contentment. Every now and then one would walk off, strut up and down for a few seconds and then flop on to the sand. I did not stay long because they were clearly about to set off on their night's hunting, and the presence of the vehicle might hamper them.

Though I had not yet found Temba and Tombi I was in an optimistic mood. For one thing, that day I had smelt the approach of winter, and here this season is the most magnificent of the year, the time when the bush is brown and dry and arid–looking, and I love it like that. Winter also meant that from now on the lions would be a lot less difficult to find because the rivers dry up and the game is forced to use the perennial springs and the few manmade water holes within their range. Where game was, predators, too, would be. I felt so elated that evening that I announced that I had not even given up hope of finding Agamemnon again. But Jack shook his head sadly. 'No,' he said. 'You won't be seeing Agamemnon again. Something dreadful has happened to him, and he is dead. I just know.'

CHAPTER 3

The Return
of the White Lions

Now that my book was beginning to earn some real money I was able for the first time to get myself properly equipped.

I had started out with a broken-down jeep which belonged to my father, a borrowed rifle and a notebook. Now I had a new diesel Land Rover, some new lenses for my camera, a spotmeter and a tape recorder. The important part the recorder was to play in my life I did not yet guess but already it was a boon, because I could keep it on the seat beside me and dictate my observations as I drove along, whereas previously, I had had to stop and take out a notebook or if I was following the lions through difficult country, I had to try to remember my impressions and make notes of them when I got back to camp.

The news that reached us at this time was not encouraging. A few days after I found Phuma's sub-group again, Keith Joubert, a wildlife artist by profession and a close friend and neighbour, told me that a nearby farmer had been shooting lions again. This man breeds cattle and, since lions are extremely partial to cattle and find them much easier to kill than wildlife, I suppose one can't blame him for shooting them. But rumour had it that, besides shooting the lions which invaded his territory, whenever my lions showed any signs of approaching his fence, as they had done on a few occasions during the rainy season, he used to kill a wildebeest or donkey, lay it out just

28

inside his boundary, and then play recordings of lions on a kill to lure them on to his land, where they would be unprotected by law, and could legally be shot as vermin. I would have to retaliate by playing tape recordings from the opposite direction, to lure them back on to their own range again. This farmer once boasted that he stopped counting when he had killed two hundred lions, and now Keith said that an African had told him the man was again shooting lions. My worry increased when I learned that about two weeks earlier my lions – including one white – had been seen in this area. This could have been Phuma and that sub-group, or part of it, but it could also have been Tabby and her cubs, and if there were only one white one, it might mean that either Temba or Tombi had been killed. However, I felt pretty certain that if there had been a white lion among those shot, the African would have mentioned it.

On 26 March, I went out in the Land Rover and discovered that a zebra had been killed during the night. This was clearly the work of the big sub-group; so many lions had been involved that all that was left of the zebra was a clean skeleton. It was a cold, windy day, the sort of day on which the lions rarely venture out on the plains but stick to the shelter of the riverine bush, and so I only managed to catch a few random glimpses of them. But on the next day we found them lying on the edge of the alkaline plain under a shingayi tree; the weather had improved but not all the sub-group had ventured out on to the plain. Some were still huddling in the riverine bush.

We saw them again on 28 March, in the area we call The Triangle. They had killed a large wildebeest bull and had left nothing apart from the head. Something that puzzled me was that although there was nothing left on the skeleton, there were at least eight vultures perched in the nearby trees. I thought this might indicate a second kill until I saw them swooping down and collecting an object which they proceeded to eat. This turned out to be lion droppings which, because of the lion's diet are naturally very rich in protein.

On this occasion the Interloper was resting with this sub-group and appeared to be completely accepted by them, or at any rate by the cubs. They rolled all over him, and sat on his head, and he didn't even growl at them; in fact he behaved in every way as if he were a member of the pride. The two Musketeers were not with the group, and on our way home we saw them about half a mile away at Piggy Dam. What, I wondered, did this mean? Had the Interloper ousted them in an effort to take over the pride? At one stage while we were observing them, he approached one of the lionesses, Scar-leg, as if to make advances, but she growled menacingly and after standing around for a few minutes looking rather awkward, he slunk away. It seemed, therefore, that the Interloper had not yet been accepted by the Machaton lionesses as a pride male.

An interesting fact one notices when watching lions, especially during their waking up period, is the amount of physical contact that takes place between the various members of the pride. They seem to like to lie near each other, touching one another, and there is always a lot of formal greeting and cheek rubbing. Indeed they are a good deal more sociable in their habits than most groups of humans that I've met.

A lioness will walk up to another lioness of the pride, greet her warmly and flop down next to her, sometimes half on top of her. The cubs all greet the lionesses and the young males, as well as one another, and lie near them or actually on them; they remain in touch with one another all the time.

I sat in the Land Rover watching them and photographing them for at least two hours before the sun went down and they stalked away towards the black soil plains over to the west. It was glorious to see these magnificent animals trooping in single file, one after the other, across the green belt, lit by the last rays of the sun.

On Wednesday, 30 March, having driven over a hundred miles in the previous few days without so much as a glimpse of the lions, we decided to spend the night on their range, listening for roars in the hope that we could locate the white lions. 'We', in this case, included Charlotte, Robert and Keith Joubert. We were in a closed Volkswagen Combi, more comfortable for sleeping in than the Land Rover. We parked in The Triangle, halfway between the Mayem-bule and the Machaton; it was a glorious night, and unusually quiet, with a half moon.

And it was on that magical night that we found the white lions, or, to be more precise, they found us. Keith Joubert was out of the vehicle, setting up camp. He had a cylinder of butane gas and a stove on which to boil a kettle, and had moved away from the Volkswagen Combi to gather some wood to light the fire, when suddenly he flung himself back into the Combi, shouting: 'My God, there are lions out there, a whole lot of them and among them a white cub.'

The cub was only a few yards away from the Combi. It was Temba and he came right up to us. As he sniffed around the gas stove I suddenly saw a second white. Both had grown a lot since I had last seen them; in fact by now they were huge.

Tabby then appeared, chewed at the gas cylinder and sniffed at the kettle. Vela followed her, and then Dimples.

The whole group were there, just as I had first seen them in 1975. To be quite truthful they were rather too close for my comfort. I decided to ease myself into the driver's seat so that, if necessary, I could drive off in a hurry.

Very soon Tabby ran off with the kettle and then settled down to bite a hole in it. The white cubs stood out at night and I got a good view of them. They looked huge but very thin, so I promised myself that in the morning I would shoot an impala for them, if I could find one. Soon the lions went off leaving us with no hot water and no kettle and I wondered how much damage they might have done to the gas cylinder. We were not going to have any tea that night and Robert would have to do without his bottle.

Presently, the lions returned and again came right up to the car – at night they don't seem to bother about the scent of men. One of the cubs began playing like a cat with the gas cylinder and finally carried it right up to the top of an ant hill, heavy though it was.

I thought we ought to go away quickly and bring back a carcass. In the hope of inducing them to stay in this place we threw a pillow for them to play with. The lions at once made a rush for it.

We left them playing with the pillow and drove south along the Machaton in the hope of finding some impala but all we found were wildebeest, which I was reluctant to shoot because Tryg didn't want any wildebeest shot that year. Also we were beginning to run a little low on fuel, and I wanted to go back and, if the lions happened to be still there, stick with them until they settled down at dawn. We would then have the whole day to go off and shoot an impala, knowing that they would be most unlikely to move again before sundown.

Alas, when we reached the spot where they had been, it was deserted. We found the kettle, perforated in a dozen places, and the gas cylinder, covered in saliva. The white lions had disappeared as mysteriously as they had arrived.

If it were not for the chewed-up kettle and the saliva all over the gas cylinder, it might all have been a dream.

With Jack Mathebusa, looking for the lions *Peter Dixon*

Agamemnon, one of the Machaton pride males and father of the white lions

Temba, Tombi and Vela

Temba, the male white cub

his sister, Tombi

Phuma, the third white cub, born to another lioness of the pride

Tabby, the mother of Temba, Tombi and Vela

Tabby and Temba, Vela in the background

Tombi with Dimples, Tabby's great friend, who broke away from the main group to live with Tabby and her cubs

Lionesses from Phuma's sub-group greeting each other

CHAPTER 4

Plans for Owl Camp

Having found the lions I decided to spend the next day rigging a temporary cage around the Land Rover, using some fence poles and a bit of an old iron bedstead. It didn't look very elegant but, like the cage on my original jeep, it gave us a spurious feeling of safety.

The following night we parked at Elephant Valley Dam, just as the sun went down. We could see a gaggle of Egyptian geese, some francolin, three rhino, at least fifty wildebeest and about the same number of zebra, many kudu and some impala. It is hard to believe that not so long ago, apart from the equatorial forests and the deserts, the whole of Africa was filled with wildlife; the taming of the European landscape has taken centuries. In Africa it has been achieved, if achieved is the right word, in a few generations.

This was another fruitless night; we didn't even hear any roars which might have indicated to us where the lions were. It's a curious thing, but since the disappearance of the pride males, there has been far less roaring at night. They used to roar fairly consistently, and the lionesses frequently roared back in response, so that we could always tell roughly where the two sub-groups might be found. The virtual cessation of roaring at night made them far harder to find and offered yet another illustration of the role the males play in maintaining the integrity of the pride. What I couldn't understand was why no strange nomads seemed to have made any effort to expropriate this magnificent range and the highly desirable females that go with it.

The next morning we went out again, to see if we could find a sign of the white cubs. We came upon some spoor near my father's camp going in the direction of the danger fence; it looked like that of Tabby, Dimples and the three cubs, a further indication that they were sticking to the extreme south-western fringe of the range.

We spent the morning following up the usual clues; like a detective one follows up every slightest hint, knowing that most of them will lead nowhere, but knowing too that it is often the most unpromising lead that will produce results.

For example, we saw three or four vultures flying in a fixed direction and roared after them in case they had seen a kill, only to discover that what they were heading for was a thermal – a rising current of warm air. When we got there, there were about twenty vultures using this lift to gain height. When they had gained sufficient height, they would cruise around all day, so high that they were not even visible from the ground, though their own eyesight is keen enough to enable them to spot anything below that looks interesting.

That evening we were out again; Charlotte and Robert, Keith Joubert and Petri Viljoen. The smoke from the camp fire rose straight into the air and visibility was excellent because there was a very bright moon and plenty of reflected light from the sandy plains.

Petri had been to the Kruger National Park to try to get some more information about their culling programme. Apparently they had been culling lions on a regular basis since November, in that part of the Kruger which shares a common fence with Timbavati, so it seemed likely that this is how Agamemnon met his end. Their reason for culling the lions was that they hoped thereby to increase the wildebeest and zebra, an approach which from my point of view is pure nonsense. There has never been any firm evidence that killing predators increases the numbers of their prey species, but it has sometimes happened that a culling programme has been followed coincidentally by an increase in the numbers of prey animals, and the wrong conclusions have been drawn. What worried me was that the many private reserves in the area usually took their lead from the Kruger.

Tryg Cooper had brought over a prominent wildlife expert who promised to get hold of a radio collar and some radio-telemetry equipment for me. They would be useful because I could then dart one of the lionesses and, while she was unconscious, fit the collar. After that I would be able to trace her movements continuously. A programme of darting and marking lions was shortly to start in the Sabie Sands private reserve about sixty miles from us, and I decided to go and see how it was done.

That night I was again out alone in the Land Rover. I heard a kudu alarm call and searched the area thoroughly because these animals don't give alarm calls for nothing, but I couldn't find anything to justify the call.

Next I heard a wildebeest: not an alarm call this time, but a territorial noise, like a great big contented belch. People often ask me why it is that these prey animals persist in making their noisy territorial calls which must draw attention to themselves and indicate to the lions where they are to be found.

I think the answer is that it's another indication of the relatively minor role which predation plays in their lives and shows that natural selection has found it unnecessary to eliminate territorial noises, even though they must attract predators. In other words, in the survival of the wildebeest as a species, territorial behaviour and all that it implies, such as honking at night, seems to play a more vital role in ensuring their survival as a species than avoiding predation.

If you take the Machaton pride, I suspect that there has been a similar pride of lions using this range, generation after generation, for thousands, maybe millions, of years, and that their numbers, with minor variations, have never multiplied to such an extent that they ever seriously interfered with the environment. If this had happened, they would have wiped out their prey species and would themselves have become extinct – from starvation. In the event, the entire ecosystem has maintained itself without degenerating.

As I sat in the Land Rover I saw some car lights coming down the Line Road, and assumed that it was somebody out looking for the white lions, or possibly poachers. I got my rifle ready because there are some pretty rough characters around here; not that I intended to shoot them, but they were quite likely to take a pot shot at me and, if this happened, I planned to put a bullet through the engine.

But it turned out to be Charlotte and Petri, with a friend of his called Warwick Tarboton, who also works for the Division of Nature Conservation. Warwick was anxious to make a study of our alkaline and black soil plains. Petri asked me to leave off watching for the lions for that night, get back to the camp, have some rest, and then take Warwick out to see the plains in the morning.

I agreed, and at first light on Saturday 7 April we set out for Elephant Valley where we immediately ran into Temba, Tombi and Vela with Tabby and Dimples. They were looking very sleek and well-fed, so for the time being I didn't have to worry about feeding them artificially; obviously Tabby and Dimples were still looking after them. Warwick was amazed at the whiteness of the lions. He hadn't really believed me when I told him that they were pure white; before the first colour pictures of them were published, nobody did.

The story of the white lions was to be released on 9 May. Pictures – both stills and movies – were to be issued simultaneously on both sides of the Atlantic, and the story was to be syndicated in a number of newspapers and magazines all over the world.

On our way back to Timbavati, I made a decision. In fact, it was a decision I had taken a long time earlier, but until the money started to come in, I hadn't been able to implement it. I had, however, discussed it with Charlotte and she had agreed with me.

We would leave our job as soon as possible and devote all our time and attention to the lions. Apart from the fact that looking after the camp and its guests took up most of our days, the camp was nine or ten miles from the part of the range now being used by Tabby and her cubs, so we were wasting a lot of time and fuel travelling back and forwards to the fringe of the lions' territory. A couple of the owners had offered us the use of their camps on a temporary basis but, as they used them from time to time throughout the year, this was no permanent solution and, in any event, we wanted to live right in the bush, as far away from human habitation as possible.

Originally, I had planned to buy or rent a trailer caravan but I soon realised that no caravan large enough to offer any degree of comfort would be capable of negotiating the dry river beds, some of which have almost perpendicular banks. We discussed living in tents, but that could only be a temporary measure because we always had a constant stream of visitors, and after the release of the news of the white lions there were likely to be a lot more, and you can't really sit down and entertain visitors in a tent.

So, gradually, the plans were formed for what was later to be known as Camp Owl. It was called Camp Owl for two reasons. One was that the initials stand for Operation White Lion which was what the whole thing was about – an operation designed to save the world's only white lions. The other was that the locals had now started to call me *Isikova*, which means owl in Zulu, because, like the owl, I spent my nights out in the bush and my days asleep in bed.

We would have to get permission from one of the owners to build the camp on his land, but I didn't anticipate any problems there. Nick Hancock had already offered me the use of his camp and would have no objection, I felt sure, to my building a little camp of my own on the edge of his land, near the Kruger Park fence.

Both Charlotte and I wanted to keep everything as simple as possible. Even a paraffin lamp has to be trimmed and cleaned and adjusted, but nothing can go wrong with a candle – you just strike a match and you've got all the light you need. My philosophy has always been total simplicity. It doesn't work, of course, once you start getting involved with Land Rovers and tape recorders and cameras and exposure meters, but as far as the camp itself was concerned I was determined to keep it as simple as was humanly possible. An outer palisade of logs and reeds, with an opening which could be closed at night. (This wouldn't keep out a determined elephant, but then neither would a brick wall.) Inside this palisade we would have a mud hut, built on the traditional African pattern: a basic framework of wood, thick, heavy clay for the walls, clay for the floor and thatch for the roof. Very cool, with tiny windows. I lived in one in Botswana for months and felt completely at home in it – it's the way I like to live. We'd get water from a windmill, so that there wouldn't be any messing about with a diesel pump. A rifle and some ammunition would ensure our supply of meat. As far as other things are concerned, it would be a question of going into Hoed-spruit every couple of weeks to stock up. We would make a lot of biltong because in this situation we'd be forced to live on it a good part of the time. Fresh biltong, made from impala, is nothing more than strips of raw meat cured in the air and the sunshine; when it's about a week old it tastes exactly like that smoked beef you pay the earth for in fashionable restaurants.

We would have a three-legged pot, and we'd leave that over a fire in the middle of the enclosure, with one or two logs under it so that it would keep simmering gently, and we'd have a big stew on the go and keep adding to it, so that it would be there all the time – in fact it would get more tasty after the first few days – and anybody who felt hungry could just get a cup and dip into the pot. We didn't plan on a regular schedule of fixed meal-times; we would go on to the lions' schedule. After about ten days, the stew would begin to get gungy, then we would throw it out and start all over again: what could be simpler than that?

Inside the palisade we would have another screen and behind that a couple of tents for overnight guests and for Tabs and Robert to sleep in. I'd have another tent, outside the palisade and away from the noise of the children, as my office. There I would sort out my slides, keep my camera equipment and make my notes and check through the tape recordings.

For sanitation we'd have what is known in these parts as a 'long drop' – a lavatory seat over a deep hole in the ground, with a screen around it; not all the way around though, because Charlotte said she had always wanted a loo with a view. The long drop would be outside the palisade, naturally. In time we would go in for such minor luxuries as a kerosene fridge (a near necessity to keep meat fresh in hot weather) and a hot and cold shower: a Heath Robinson contraption involving two forty-four-gallon petrol drums, one with a wood fire under it. Initially, for baths, we would use an old tin bath, in front of the fire.

If possible we would build the camp near Jack Mathebula's house because, as he is the best tracker I've ever worked with, I would be needing his help to keep in touch with my lions now that Tabby and her sub-group had been banished from the core of the range and were only very rarely to be seen in their favourite and familiar resting places.

The moment we arrived back in Timbavati I went out looking for the lions and saw something that disturbed me more than anything had done since the disappearance of Agamemnon. I observed Tabby and Dimples with two of the Musketeers. There was no sign of the white cubs. During my absence Petri hadn't seen them. And now that the whole world knew about the white lions of Timbavati, there was nothing to stop anybody from luring them into the regions west of Timbavati, beyond the danger fence, darting them and capturing them for sale to a zoo or a circus.

I tried to think back to the time when the original three Musketeers and Suzie Wong were about the same age as Temba, Tombi and Vela. Their mother, Golden, had deserted them from time to time, initially for brief periods which gradually increased in length as she became ready to breed again and started to lose interest in them. When she finally left them to their own devices, they attached themselves for a time to Tabby and her cubs, and she and Dimples did their hunting for them. Tabby's own cubs were by then so big that the Musketeers no longer represented a menace to them. Any menace that is, in the sense that older cubs can easily injure young ones on a kill; but later, when they became pride males, the Musketeers would constitute a threat of a far more sinister kind.

If Tabby was now ready to breed again and prepared to desert her cubs, the trio had no sub-group to which they could attach themselves until they were sufficiently skilled to make their own kills. The seven cubs of the main sub-group were all still so young that Tabby's cubs would have represented a menace to them on a kill, and consequently there was no chance that those four lionesses would let Temba, Tombi and Vela anywhere near their cubs, much less hunt for them. Also, since our cubs were living on the very fringe of the range, they were exposed to many other dangers.

I asked Jack what he thought had happened. He wasn't perturbed: 'I haven't any tremendous feelings of worry or anxiety about them,' he said. 'I don't have any "earth feelings" that they're not here any longer, as I had with Agamemnon. I just think perhaps they're sleeping near a kill or lying up somewhere in the bush. They're safe, wherever they are. I feel certain of that.'

'Wherever they are' – that was the problem, for we had lost them a second time.

CHAPTER 5

Search from the Air

Although as a scientist, there was no reason why I should have been reassured by Jack's 'earth feelings', as he calls them, that the white lions were safe, he has been right so often in the past that I have come to trust his bush instinct far more than my own judgement, and so, illogically, I did feel reassured.

But if Tabby and Dimples were on heat again and had started to leave the three cubs for longer or shorter periods while they went off flirting with young males, this was going to make my job a lot more difficult. Without Tabby and Dimples to hunt for them and to protect them, the cubs were going to remain hidden most of the time in the thick riverine bush; they were not going to use any of the old familiar routes or resting places, even assuming they knew how to find them. So I'd have to start spooring again, on foot if necessary. It also meant that as soon as we found them we would need to feed them.

The fact that the Musketeers and the Interloper were still in residence seemed to support the theory that Agamemnon was dead and that Achilles, for his own good reasons, had permanently transferred his allegiance to the adjoining Velvet Paws pride. It also seemed to indicate that the Musketeers and the Interloper were beginning to be accepted by the Machaton lionesses as pride males, a fact which pleased me greatly, since the Musketeers were almost certainly sons of Agamemnon (indeed one of them looked exactly like a younger version of him) and therefore might be expected to carry the white gene. The chances of further white cubs would obviously be enormously enhanced if both the mother and father carried the same wayward gene; indeed a mating between either of the Musketeers and Tombi or even Phuma would be very likely to produce another generation of white lions.

The most urgent problem was to locate the two whites and Vela again but, as this was going to be very difficult, I decided to try first to make sure that all was still well with Phuma and the big sub-group.

I set out, about half-past five, on the morning of Sunday, 24 April. Charlotte, who had been up most of the night with Robbie, decided not to come with me, so I was on my own in the bush with only my rifle, my camera and my tape recorder for company.

I didn't have very far to drive before I came across the sub-group at Elephant Valley Dam. The two Musketeers, who had been with Tabby and Dimples the previous day, were now with this sub-group, and Phuma was looking very healthy, though not perhaps quite as snowy white as the other two. The four lionesses, Golden, Scarleg, Greta, Suzie Wong were drinking at the dam, along with seven cubs. Shortly Lona, obviously lactating, came out of the bush and joined them; clearly she had some very young cubs hidden somewhere in the thickest part of the bush and, as I never saw any sign of her offspring subsequently, it is probable that they died in infancy, a very common occurrence among lions. Lionesses normally keep their cubs hidden somewhere in the bush until they are a couple of months old and will not allow anyone to approach them. Tabby had been an unusually casual mother in not showing the slightest objection to our observing and even photographing her unique cubs when they were only about a couple of weeks old.

As I watched them and the sun grew steadily in strength, the lions one by one settled down to sleep and, as I knew that they would stay there until sundown, I felt free to go off and look for Tabby's family.

I dropped into Mandaban's house to see whether he had seen or heard anything of them. He wasn't there when I arrived but there was a pot of biltong stew on the fire, so I helped myself. Then I had a short sleep during the hottest part of the day when the lions too would have been sleeping.

I was awakened by Mandaban's return. He had heard some lions roaring the previous night from the direction of the Mayembule and we both thought that they were probably Tabby's sub-group. I left at three o'clock and drove along the east bank of the Mayembule, then crossed through the dry river bed and drove all the way along the left bank. There was no sign of the white lions. In order not entirely to waste the day, I then returned to Elephant Valley Dam, where Phuma's sub-group was just beginning to wake up. I took some photographs and stayed with the lions until twenty minutes after dusk – by then the light was much too weak for any further photography.

As I drove off, a couple of cubs followed the car, stalking it as they stalk rhino, but after a few hundred yards they flopped down in the sand, rolled over and had another rest, before setting off hunting with the lionesses.

One of the standard methods of attracting lions in the game parks (for the purpose of darting them, either to capture them or to treat them for disease, or merely to mark them for subsequent identification) is by playing recordings of predators on a kill. Hyena tapes are the most commonly used and are the most effective because hyena are extremely noisy on a kill, laughing and cackling in a maniacal manner that carries over vast distances in the silent bush. Tapes of lions on a kill are also used but they are less effective. One reason for this may be that while lions know perfectly well that they will be capable of chasing a few hyenas from their kill and stealing it for themselves, they are by no means so certain of being able to horn in on another pride's feast, or even on a kill made by a sub-group of the same pride. So, one reason why the cackling of hyenas on a kill normally gets results is because, being extremely lazy animals, any lions within earshot will almost invariably come running up to the source of the noise on the chance of a free meal.

I now decided to try out tapes in the hope of luring the white lions out of the thick bush. I knew that John Dunning had been using this technique to observe and photograph lions for many years so I now asked him to lend me some of his tapes. In the meantime, I continued to drive around the range, day after day, night after night, hoping to stumble across the whites by chance. But although I saw Phuma's sub-group again and again, there was no trace of Temba and Tombi, nor did I again see Tabby and Dimples fraternising with the Musketeers. This was a good sign.

When not out searching, I tried to learn as much as I could from Petri about the technique for darting lions. It was clear to me that we were going to have to dart some at least of our lions pretty soon, either to fit them with a radio transmitting device so that we could monitor their movements, or in order to capture them and transfer them to safety.

The 'dart' used is a sort of hypodermic syringe. Various drugs are employed; the most common was Sernalyn, an anaesthetic. The lions are rendered completely helpless. Normally a tranquilliser is then injected to calm them during the process of capture and transportation, or while they are being treated by a vet, or tagged.

The needle of the dart or syringe is barbed, so that the animal cannot shake it out before the drug has been injected. The actual injection is achieved by a small explosive charge in the dart, which detonates on impact and shoots the plunger forward, forcing the drug into the animal. The amount of drug used is critical: if you use too little, the animal may not be completely immobilised; if you use too much, the drug may cause breathing to cease. A table of doses has been worked out based on the weight of the animal being darted and, as the weight of a lion is roughly related to its age, if you know the exact age of the lions you are darting, you can be reasonably sure of getting the right dosage, though obviously mistakes can be made. During his first darting exercises at Sabie Sands, Petri underestimated the weight of a young male lion, one with a very small, short mane, but it was a lot heavier than he thought – 411 pounds in fact – so the drug didn't immobilise him completely.

The dart is fired from a gun or a pistol. At close range a gun that works by gas pressure is used, because the pressure can be varied according to the distance, but if you are obliged to dart the lions from some considerable distance, a gun with an explosive charge is used. Hand pistols, also worked by gas cylinders or compressed air, are mainly used in zoos to dart animals which have escaped from their cages.

Since the lions in our area are nocturnal, it is only possible to use the hyena tapes to call them up at night, which adds greatly to the problem of darting them. The drug does not act instantaneously; sometimes the lions run for quite a distance before they drop, and are often extremely difficult to find at night in the thick bush. In addition there is always the danger that the lion, when you do find him, has not been completely immobilised, or that the tape recordings of the hyena calls have attracted the attention of other lions in the area which haven't been darted and of whose presence you were unaware. All round it's a pretty dangerous operation, both for the lions and the human beings involved, but nobody has so far come up with a more effective technique.

The amplifier used to broadcast the tapes is a very powerful one, giving a range, to the human ear, of about three kilometres, though with lions it seems to work up to about seven kilometres. Therefore, as well as borrowing the tapes, I was going to have to borrow or hire a powerful amplifier and speakers to give me the necessary range, since my small portable tape recorder would be quite inadequate. To set all this up would take some time. Meanwhile the need to find the cubs was urgent.

I decided that the circumstances jusitifed the expense of an air search and got in touch with the pilot of a light plane in Phalaborwa, hired him for a day and gave him directions which I hoped would be adequate to enable him to pick out a nearby airstrip in Timbavati, about five miles from our lodge.

With Chris Bowling, a writer friend who lives at White River, I went out to look at the airstrip. There were quite a few giraffe on it, which we chased away, before examining the surface of the strip. There were some fairly fresh hollows on the runway, where the wildebeest had been wallowing; we also found a new ant heap which we proceeded to flatten. By the time we had finished that job the giraffes had wandered back on to the strip, and had to be sent packing.

As soon as we had everything in fairly good shape, Charlotte drove up and told us that a message had just come through that the pilot was not arriving until the following day. I wasn't surprised – that's Africa. Nothing ever happens on the day it's supposed to happen; indeed you can count yourself lucky if it happens at all.

Rather than waste the rest of the day we spent six hours driving around the bush looking for the white lions – without success. During the evening, I began to wonder whether the pilot would find the airstrip as it isn't marked on any of the maps. We sat outside the *rondavel*, discussing the question. It was a beautiful night, with a full moon, and there was so little wind that I was able to relight my pipe without cupping my hands around the flame of the match. It wasn't hot and it wasn't cold – quite warm enough for us to sit out in shirtsleeves, but not so hot that sleeping would be difficult. No mosquitoes, no insects – the perfect life . . .

Chris Bowling and I decided that although the instructions I had given the pilot were definite he mightn't recognise the airstrip as such because from the air it didn't look very much less wild than the surrounding bush. To guide him we hit upon the brilliant plan of getting as many of the team as we could muster down on to the airstrip at the appropriate time, all waving Robbie's freshy laundered white nappies – no pilot could miss this dazzling display.

The next morning we were all out on the tarmac as planned and at precisely the estimated time of arrival we heard the drone of an aeroplane engine and realised that the pilot had seen the strip and was very wisely circling it before attempting to land. Soon he made a neat, if slightly bumpy, landing and rolled to a stop.

We set off, almost immediately. I travelled in the plane with the pilot and Chris Bowling, while Charlotte, Tabs and Keith Joubert did a search on the ground in the Land Rover.

The plane was a single-engined Cessna. Running up for the takeoff was a bit hair-raising because of all the holes the wildebeest had made along the runway. In spite of this, the pilot was able to get up enough airspeed to limp into the air and, as soon as we were airborne, he headed for the Machaton river; our plan was to start by flying its whole length.

The rains had come and gone and the river beds were as dry as a bone – pale yellow snakes of sand winding their way through the still bright green riverine bush, which draws its moisture from the water table far below the surface. The landscape was curious – a flat, dry, burnt-out savannah, and a lot of dead, whitening skeletons of trees pushed over and uprooted by the elephants, as well as the skeletons of the predators' kills.

It was not in the ordinary sense beautiful or picturesque, and yet to me it was the most beautiful place in the world. That could be because I was born in South Africa and had spent a lot of the formative years of my life walking in the lowveld with Jack, the tracker, and my father.

There's a phrase they use a lot down here, which I suppose could be applied to me: 'bush happy'. It is applied to people like myself who are only completely happy wandering about in the bush and, if it implies a kind of madness, I'd rather be bush happy than preoccupied with the performance of my sports car or my hi-fi.

At first I found it extremely difficult to spot any of the wildlife from the plane. The dry river beds I recognised immediately, and even the breaks in the riverine vegetation through which we constantly used to drive the Land Rover to reach the river banks. I was struck again, as I always am, whenever I fly over the territory, by the way in which even a light plane such as a Cessna can swallow up distances: in a few minutes we had covered an area that would have taken me several hours to negotiate in the Land Rover, and a whole, long, weary day on foot. I was also, as usual, amazed by the curious miniaturisation effect that flying produces: it is like looking at a familiar landscape through the wrong end of a pair of binoculars.

From a point roughly above Jack's house, we suddenly caught sight of some lions. They looked to me like members of the Velvet Paws pride. So we circled again to make sure. On the second circuit I was quite sure that these were the Velvet Paws. I decided that we would do a check from the ground because I wanted to find out whether the big male with them was Achilles.

Almost immediately afterwards, we came across Phuma's subgroup, but still there was no sign of the other whites. After about an hour and a half in the air, we returned to the landing strip. Another fruitless search had ended. This was getting monotonous.

That morning we had flown up and down the Machaton, then around the fringe of the range, then away outside this fringe in case some of our lions had wandered off into the Kruger National Park and then all along the western fringe, in fact along all the fringes. Finally we had flown in ever-decreasing circles towards the centre of the range. It was only towards the end of the flight that I began to be able to pick out lions at all, because they lie in the shade and they are extremely well camouflaged.

When, after lunch, we tried to take off again, we found a whole troop of baboons on the runway and had to chase them off before we could start up the plane. They loped into the trees surrounding the runway and perched there awaiting events and watching us with interest, while we started our run-up to the take-off point. They are very intelligent creatures; in fact I'm not sure that we shouldn't give them a seat in the United Nations.

The light was much better this time and my eyes had become accustomed to observing the wildlife from about a hundred feet up. I saw a single warthog almost immediately after take-off, so there was no reason why I shouldn't see the white lions unless . . . This was what I didn't want to think about, because it would mean that Jack was wrong and they had disappeared.

This part of Africa is a maze of game parks, all primeval land, largely untouched by man since the first days of the world, which is what makes it feel so strange to look down on it in this god-like fashion from a flying machine. I couldn't help feeling it was sheer impertinence.

We saw the Velvet Paws pride and a big male, undoubtedly Achilles.

During one hour we covered the entire range for the second time, flying backwards and forwards in every conceivable combination of directions but we still didn't see any lions that looked remotely like Tabby and the whites.

As we came in, there was a wildebeest lying right in the middle of the landing strip and we had to fly over him, dead low, to frighten him out of his wits and then make a wide turn and come back in again before he had time to return to what was obviously one of his favourite wallowing spots.

Charlotte now thought up another plan. She drove around the whole area calling on the local Shangaans and offering fifteen rand and a bottle of brandy to anybody who could find the white lions and lead us to them. She confidently expected that by the following morning there would be at least twenty people out searching the bush. That they would find the whites was a slender hope, but twenty pairs of eyes are better than two or three and she thought the Shangaans would put themselves to a great deal of trouble if a bottle of brandy were to be part of the contract.

CHAPTER 6

Mandaban
Sees the White Lions

The next day I set out very early, and spent three hours walking through the bush with Jack Mathebula, the tracker, looking for spoor. We did find some lion spoor but again it was Phuma's sub-group.

In the meantime, Charlotte and Pamela, Chris Bowling's wife, went out on their own in a clapped-out old Land Rover. They went off, as Pamela put it, 'determined to think positive thoughts and scan every plain we could find, leaving no bush unturned'.

Charlotte, who had been listening to Jack, still had a strong feeling that the white lions were somewhere in the area of my father's farm, so they went first in that direction. As they were driving along they came across some spoor which looked about right for the white cubs, but it was at least a day old. As the spoor was leading in the direction of Vlak, they carried on towards my father's farm. There was no one there so they drove to the Lily Pan on my uncle Rob's farm. Incidentally, no one ever planted the lilies which gave that pan its name; the seeds must have been carried there by birds.

On the way to the pan, they saw the remains of a wildebeest kill, fresh that night, with Mandaban standing beside it with his bicycle. They stopped the Land Rover and asked him what had happened, because when they have thoroughly gorged themselves lions normally sleep, right beside the kill.

Mandaban told them he had seen the lions on the kill earlier that morning: eight in all, including the two whites. He had not heard about the reward because he had been missing from his *kraal* when Charlotte made her rounds.

'Are you sure, Mandaban, absolutely sure?' Charlotte asked. 'Oh, yes, it was them all right.'

Eight lions: that would be Tabby, Dimples, the three cubs, Temba, Tombi and Vela and three others, probably the two Musketeers and the Interloper. What had happened to frighten them off the kill? Of course they could still be resting in the bush somewhere nearby.

Mandaban threw his bicycle into the Land Rover and before long they picked up the spoor and started tracking them from the vehicle, Mandaban sitting on the bonnet and sometimes walking ahead. At a certain point he suddenly said, 'You are going to find them around here', and at that moment they noticed Mrs Marula, Moskyn's wife, scurrying through the bush. She made no attempt to greet them, which was unusual, so they assumed that she had been up to her old tricks, chasing the lions off their kill and stealing the meat for herself. Mandaban had seen them on the kill at eight o'clock, so they couldn't have gone very far.

Charlotte continued to track them in the Land Rover. Mandaban got down from time to time to examine the spoor and reported it to be very fresh, and added that the lions appeared to be running, probably running away from the car. Charlotte switched off the ignition and in whispers they discussed what their next move should be. It would have been dangerous to attempt to spoor them on foot, as the bush in this area was very dense and none of them had a gun. When Charlotte tried to start up the Land Rover again, the engine refused to start. In fact they had the wrong ignition key with them, so how it had started earlier I can't imagine.

Mandaban went off on his bicycle to our lodge – a two and a half hour cycle ride – to fetch help. While they were waiting, Charlotte and Pamela walked to Rob's camp, and tried to find a screwdriver; there were no tools in the Land Rover. All they could find in his tool shed was a plastering trowel, so using that they spent a couple of hours dismantling the dashboard of the Land Rover, and joining various wires together – Pam had once lost the ignition key of a Volkswagen and had managed to start the engine by joining some wires behind the dashboard. This exercise, however, proved fruitless so they sat down under a tree. They had been out from seven o'clock in the morning, and it was after four o'clock in the afternoon before I eventually reached them. They had had nothing to eat except one rusk each and a drink of very murky water from a tap beside Rob's pan. At first they were happy enough sitting in the sun, but eventually they began to worry about the children, assuming, rightly as it proved, that Chris and I were probably out looking for the lions in the new Land Rover. There was a swimming pool at the camp, and the Africans who were looking after the four children – our two and the Bowlings' pair – don't like the water and cannot swim, so Charlotte and Pam were picturing the children face-down in the water and various other unpleasant situations. Also, they had just run over and killed a snake. They were both very nervous of snakes and they were in an area where snakes of all sorts abound, and they had no anti-snake serum. So it had been quite an ordeal for them.

When Chris Bowling and I came to rescue them in our new Land Rover, we brought all four children with us. Eventually we got the old Land Rover started by putting the correct wires together and fastening them in place with a plastic bag we had in one of the vehicles. We then went off to try to follow the spoor of the whites, leaving Charlotte and Pam to take the children home. On the way the wires kept coming loose and Pam had to hold them together while Charlotte drove through the bush without lights because the battery was too flat to keep the engine going with the lights on. Every time they went over a bump, Pam let the wires go and the engine conked out and had to be started again. As if this were not enough, the steering was so loose that they kept running into trees. Both of them agreed that it was the worst drive of their lives.

In the meantime, Chris and I searched the area thoroughly and although we found the spoor, we saw no sign of the lions.

However, the picture was a little brighter than it had been a day earlier when the air search had drawn a total blank. Mandaban remained adamant that he had seen Temba, Tombi and Vela and I had no reason to disbelieve him.

Still, my mind would not be completely at rest until I had actually seen the whites with my own eyes. I felt a great deal happier, but I would have felt even happier if it had been Jack and not Mandaban who had told Charlotte that he had seen the lions. With Jack, I would have been one hundred per cent convinced; with Mandaban, let's say the figure was around ninety per cent.

Friday, 6 May was my birthday and Chris Bowling and I spent it sleeping out, listening for lion roars. We heard only one, and that was early in the morning. It was only a low moan and didn't last long enough for us to get out of the cab and try to fix the direction from which it had come. So we fetched Mandaban and walked in a wide circle in the hope that we would find some fresh spoor. The first we saw was the previous day's spoor and it was clear that the lions had run a long way from the point where they had been disturbed by Mrs Marula. We would never have found them the previous day before dark. This morning they appeared to be making towards the Mayembule River, and rather than track them on foot, which might have disturbed them again, we decided to go after them in the Land Rover. There are a few water holes where the game congregate *en route* and we took a close look at all of these as we passed by. But once, again, it proved a futile operation so we decided to knock off after driving from four o'clock in the morning until noon.

At least I think I achieved one thing. I had a long and very earnest discussion with Mrs Marula in the course of which I tried, through a combination of urgent persuasion, veiled threats and vague bribes, to extract from her a promise never again to chase the white lions off a kill and steal their meat. From our examination of the spoor, Mandaban and I realised just how far away they had run from where they had been resting after the kill. They had been lying right next to it before Mrs Marula arrived and we could have found them easily if she hadn't chased them off.

A few days later we were delighted to hear that the lodge owner had found a couple of people who were prepared to take over our jobs at the camp. This meant that soon we could begin to build our own camp and concentrate on looking for – and after – the white lions.

Now that it seemed that the white cubs were still alive, I began to make a plan for feeding them regularly in some remote site probably on Vlakgesicht. My fear was that as soon as the veldt began to dry up, the cubs would go more and more often to Piggy Dam in search of game and thereby be exposed to visitors and their cameras. I thought I would establish a feeding station somewhere close to the Lily Pan, which is on the far side of the Reserve from the danger fence.

I was basically against the idea of feeding the lions artificially, but I couldn't see any other solution to the current dilemma. I still had to get more hyena tapes and the amplifying equipment we needed to attract the lions to the Land Rover; when they arrived we would feed them regularly and condition them to being fed from it. But first, we had to find them.

One day, Petri arrived with samples of tapes from John Dunning, and we had an opportunity to try them out. They included both hyenas and lions on a kill, and some territorial roaring, as well as recordings of jackal, so there was quite a selection.

The recordings of a pride of lions on a kill was particularly interesting. There was a lot of growling, a continual low rumbling, and now and again some slightly higher-pitched sounds from the cubs. Listening to the tape, it was very easy to visualise just what was going on. The lions lying there, flank to flank, growling and snarling as the young ones tried to slip in to sneak a bite. We knew only too well that if a young one managed to grab some meat, a paw would shoot out and that would be the end of the cub. Usually his back would be broken or he would suffer some other fatal injury. In fact, cubs on a kill are constantly getting clobbered and this is one of the main reasons for the high cub mortality rate.

We all enjoyed ourselves hugely listening to the tapes, but they didn't attract any lions that night.

Around that time I had been seeing Phuma's sub-group almost every day. I think this was because they had taken over the core of the range and were using all the old familiar routes and resting-places, which I kept passing, while the whites were now in a part of the range which was unfamiliar to them. It would be tedious to go through all the days and nights I now spent searching for them. From time to time Jack and I came across their spoor and on some occasions saw the remains of kills almost certainly made by them, or rather made by Tabby or Dimples on their behalf, so, obviously they were still being fed by the two lionesses. Mandaban heard them roaring several times near my father's farm, and had no doubt the whites were safe and well.

Meanwhile, the Interloper and the two Musketeers appeared to be gaining acceptance as pride males; one morning I saw one of the Musketeers marking a tree. This is a sign of territorial behavior and was one more proof that they were in the process of taking over the Machaton pride.

One of my regular chores was to shoot impala for the pot. I don't enjoy it; it's simply a job that has got to be done. Normally I use a .22 rifle and aim for the top of the head. This has the advantage that you don't damage any of the meat and also, if your aim is not dead on, the shot goes right over the top of the animal's head without injuring it.

Many people who live in towns are against hunting. If they were logical and honest about it, they would have to become vegetarians, because there is no essential difference in killing an animal for food in an abattoir, and killing one for food in the wild. Shooting animals for the sake of their hides and tusks and fur is another matter, and if done on a large commercial scale can certainly endanger a species.

Recently, there has been a change of attitude among conservationists on the subject of hunting. In the past, the preservationists tended to have an emotional outlook on hunting, regarding it as one of the major causes of the disappearance of various game species. They were convinced that if you could stop the shooting of these species, you would ensure their survival. This is not true.

In South Africa the high veldt used to be crawling with all kinds of antelope and buck, none of which now survive. But the reason for their disappearance has little or nothing to do with the fact that they were hunted; because the land on which they once lived is now being used for other purposes. It is the destruction of the animals' natural habitat which has caused the disappearance of so many species of wildlife. An old man who lives not far from my father's house in Morningside, a suburb of Johannesburg, told me that his father used to shoot lions there. The fact that there are no longer any lions in Morningside is not due to this man's father and many others having shot lions in the area; it is because Morningside is now a modern suburb with roads and houses and cars and buses and crowds of people, no longer the sort of habitat in which lions could live. This same man told me that, in his own lifetime, whenever they wanted a springbok for the Sunday dinner all they had to do was to drive about five miles out of Morningside and they would find plenty of wildlife to shoot. But today this, too, is a built-up area, a suitable habitat for man, but not for springbok. Now you would need to travel four or five hundred miles out of Johannesburg to find a springbok, except in places where they have been artificially reintroduced on private farms. Certainly there is no more effective way of rendering an animal extinct than by using its habitat for farming or mining or manufacturing or some other human activity.

On the other hand, hunting, organised on a proper basis, can actually increase the numbers of wildlife in certain areas. In Germany, for example, as far as numbers are concerned – sheer numbers as opposed to varieties of species – there is more wildlife per hectare than there is in the whole of South Africa. They do not have so large an area of national parks but they do have a long tradition of controlled hunting, and it is precisely because so much of the parkland and forest area in Germany is administered by hunting organisations that there exists this profusion of wildlife.

In America, too, they have now very many more deer than existed at any previous time in the history of the continent. There are many millions of hunters in the States – indeed hunting is a major industry – but there is a system whereby part of the revenue derived from the sale of arms and ammunition and from hunting licences is ploughed back into conservation, into research projects, for example, designed to increase the carrying capacity, in terms of wildlife, of particular tracts of land.

The problem of conservation is simply one of pressure on the limited amount of land available, and the only argument that any government would accept for preserving places like Timbavati, instead of 'developing' them, would be if we could prove that we could make them profitable; if we could demonstrate that by preserving a completely natural ecosystem, we would also be making the most efficient and profitable use of the land in terms of the production of red meat. Researchers vary in their estimates; some say that by 'farming' game species instead of cattle, it is possible to get four times as much red meat per unit area. I have seen the estimate put as high as twenty times as much, but this is probably an exaggeration. Nevertheless, it seems only common-sense that if you have an area covered with a certain kind of shrub which cattle will not eat, but steenbuck will eat up to x feet high, after which the kudu take over and eat all the leaves between x and y feet, and finally the giraffe browse from y feet to the top, it is surely rational to try to 'farm' them. All these animals produce valuable protein. Properly organised, these regions could be used in this way far more effectively than by trying to graze cattle in the area. Also, the land would not require any 'input' in the form of direct or indirect fossil fuels, fertilisers or artificial irrigation. It is a closed system into which you don't have to put anything, except a bit of thought and organisation, and out of which, if the scheme is managed efficiently, you could get a far higher yield than from any other use to which you might put the land. You would also be conserving the wildlife which would provide a tourist attraction, which in turn could be exploited to increase the profitability of the area. Finally a useful spin-off would be that the areas could also be used for scientific research by ecologists from all over the world.

Some people would object to what they would describe as the organisation of the wild into meat factories. It may be true that wild areas are essential to man's spiritual well-being but they are daily becoming fewer and nothing is more certain than that, if the few remaining wild places in South Africa are not soon made profitable, *and seen to be profitable*, the land will be commandeered and put to some other use which would inevitably mean the end of the wildlife.

The days passed, and still we could find no sign of Tabby and the white cubs, though we kept seeing evidence – in the form of fresh kills and spoor – that they were around, hiding somewhere, on the extreme south-western fringe of the range. As soon as I could get the amplifier and a supply of tapes, I planned to try to keep the lions in this area, by feeding them regularly in one or two places. The place wasn't my choice; it was Tabby's. For reasons best known to herself, she seemed to feel that her cubs were safer in the thick riverine bush along the Mayembule than anywhere else. From my point of view, this was ideal, except for the fact that it was too close to the lion-shooting farmer's fence. On the other hand, it was far away from the Kruger fence. It was also far away from the lodge we had been managing, which reduced the chances of any of the guests spotting the whites and photographing them.

Until now, the lions had ignored the old jeep and the new Land Rover; they had behaved as if they were invisible. I had made a temporary cage for the new vehicle; like the old one, it was more for our own peace of mind than anything else.

It now occurred to me that as soon as I started to feed the lions from the Land Rover, they would associate it with food and we would need a more secure cage. I drove into Nelspruit to have a solid metal cage fitted, with a hatch on the top through which I could stand up to take photographs. Charlotte had also decided to increase the reward for anyone who succeeded in taking us to the white lions from fifteen to thirty rand – which is quite a lot of money down here in the bush.

While I was off in Nelspruit, Charlotte took a party of guests for a drive in the Land Rover. They saw a lot of game and on the way back, as she passed Piggy Dam, she saw what looked like a log sticking out of the dam. Stopping to investigate, she found it was a baby giraffe which had got itself completely bogged down in the thick mud. It was exhausted from its efforts to extricate itself and was in grave danger of drowning in the mud. Indeed, Charlotte thought that the little animal had given up all hope of getting out and was preparing to die. She rallied the whole party, got the tow rope from the Land Rover, went into the mud up to her thighs, and managed to loop the rope around the young giraffe. Tabs went in with her and held the giraffe's head clear of the water. Charlotte then went back to the Land Rover, and by driving it very slowly, while the rest of the party held the other end of the rope, ready to release it if the giraffe looked like getting too badly entangled, managed to drag it out on to dry land. For a few minutes it lay there as if it were dead but then it suddenly staggered to its feet and raced off into the bush – a black giraffe, covered in mud.

Such an incident has happened here a number of times, and the interesting thing is that it is nearly always in man-made dams that it happens. The natural pans dry out completely hard and are perfectly safe, but the man-made pans, which are fed by windmills from boreholes, produce only a trickle of water in the dry season when the winds are light – often not enough for the animals to drink but quite enough to turn the dam into a sticky mud bath in which they get trapped.

It's yet another example of how man's attempts to solve one problem can often cause others.

CHAPTER 7

Luring the Lions

I now made tape recordings of the hyenas and lions on a kill from John Dunning's tapes and on 11 May tried them on my own tape recorder.

Within a few moments I was surrounded by lions. Unfortunately, they belonged to the wrong sub-group. I wasn't surprised since I knew they were in the vicinity.

I had set out along the Mayembule and we ran into a group of lions near my father's camp. At first I had been certain it was Tabby and her whites but then realised it was Phuma and her sub-group plus the Musketeers and the Interloper.

What a beautiful sight it was, a misty morning with the sun just rising and casting a golden glow over everything as it gradually dispersed the mist. Phuma and the cubs looked up at some birds that were flying over. Although it was misty, it was not very cold, and the lions were lying right out in the open, on the banks of the Mayembule.

The Interloper was developing a fine mane and maturing rapidly. With the help of the two Musketeers he should soon become a match for any nomadic lions that tried to take over this pride.

I had a feeling that Achilles might turn up again and try to reassert his rights over the Machaton pride. If he returned within the next month or so, he might just succeed, but if he left it much longer, I didn't think he would stand a chance against the three young lions.

Soon I was surrounded by lions – three nearly full-grown males, four lionesses, and seven cubs, one white.

They were just lying around, grooming themselves. The Interloper licked himself all over, like a big cat, then licked a paw and lazily rubbed it over his nose and cheek. There was another lioness lurking in the background at the edge of the riverine bush. For all we knew she might have some cubs hidden in it, perhaps another white one. Phuma was looking very white, much whiter than she had seemed the other day. She made a few sharp jabs with her mouth, like a dog, probably trying to catch a fly.

I was still worried about Temba and Tombi and would have to go off soon to look for them.

I had started the motor because I wanted to move in closer to get a better camera angle on the lions. One of the cubs had come right up to the Land Rover, no doubt out of sheer curiosity when he saw it move. He looked at me, standing less than five paces away. Then came the Musketeer who looked so like Agamemnon, and then Phuma who walked right up to the vehicle and sniffed. She was a lovely animal. I noticed that she had a scar on one of her back legs; evidently she had been in the wars already. Another cub also sniffed around the tyres, and then yet another one woke up. As it was a cool morning, they were not nearly as lethargic as usual at this time of day. I was only a few yards away from the main group when one of the Musketeers went into a stalk. He looked intently in the direction of the river bed. I couldn't see what it was that he had his eye on, but he probably wouldn't get it. With lions, most stalking attempts end in failure. According to Schaller, they are rarely more than about thirty-five per cent successful.

It was a beautiful day for the lions to lie out, cool enough for them to stay on the open sandy plains. When I drove off a few of the cubs looked up momentarily, before settling to sleep.

At the Lily Pan I met Mandaban and he had two pieces of news. He had just heard a kudu alarm call, quite close, and we decided to go and investigate. Also he had heard lions roaring the previous night near my father's dam and his own *kraal*, so it seemed worth taking a walk in the bush. But first I had breakfast with Mandaban – tea and biltong roasted on the coals accompanied by mealie-meal porridge, which is a sort of corn meal mash.

Afterwards we called on Mrs Marula. She had a sore arm and asked if I would send Charlotte over with some medicine. Charlotte was the unofficial bush doctor in this part of Timbavati, and all the locals had implicit faith in whatever she brought from the chemist at Hoedspruit – this usually consisted of antiseptics, antibiotics or sometimes aspirin.

Lena, one of Mrs Marula's daughters, was there and told me that the previous night when 'the moon was there' (pointing at the sky), which is the nearest she is ever prepared to go in establishing the time, she too had heard the lions roaring very close. Lena had just had a baby girl and asked Charlotte to choose a name for her. The baby was very small and much paler in colour than Lena's other children, so I suggested she should call her Phuma, which in Zulu means 'out of the ordinary'. She didn't appreciate the idea of having her daughter called after a lion, and said she would much prefer it if Charlotte would choose a name.

Lena thought there had been many lions roaring, so I began to wonder if it wasn't Phuma's sub-group which we had just seen, not far away. If the big sub-group had now started to hunt on Tongue Plain, where Tabby and Dimples seemed to have been doing their hunting over the past couple of weeks, where were Tabby and her cubs going to get their food?

Mandaban and I made our way to the little rocky hill, over the dam – where the roaring appeared to him to have come from, and crossed the river bed, towards the *kopje*. I remembered the spot well, from my childhood, for I used to come here and shoot sandgrouse with a shotgun – as they fly at a terrific speed, it's a tremendous sport.

We found the spoor without much difficulty. It was almost certainly that of the larger sub-group we had seen earlier that morning about two miles away. Two miles is quite a distance for lions to walk to find a suitable resting place, so there was a possibility that the spoor might have been that of one of the neighbouring prides. If so, this represented yet another potential danger to the whites. We therefore decided to stay on the spoor for a couple of hours until we had made certain, for it was essential for me to know everything that was going on in the lion world around the Machaton.

These lions, whichever pride they happened to belong to, were obviously hunting. It is very frustrating trying to spoor hunting lions because they keep doubling back and forwards and changing direction as they stalk their prey. After a couple of hours we had established to our satisfaction that the spoor was that of Phuma's sub-group, including the Interloper and the two Musketeers, so I went home to get some sleep before making yet another attempt to find Temba and Tombi.

That night I drove out alone, to the Mayembule, bringing with me the recordings I had made from John Dunning's tapes. My own portable tape recorder would not have a sufficient range, so I borrowed a slightly more powerful one from John Dunning to play the hyena tapes.

It was dark and several little jackals were wandering around. I knew there were several lions not far away for I had seen them in the morning and was certain that they had not yet moved off for the hunt. I played the tape and it worked. Soon the lions were all around the car and a low rumbling sound that was absolutely terrifying came from the left. It was a throaty roar straight from the stomach.

One of the Musketeers showed up in my headlights, surrounded by other members of the pride. They were such glorious animals I felt I could spend the rest of my life watching them, and they were so close I could hear the dry grass crackling under their paws.

My only worry was that should anything go wrong I had not got the big rifle with me. In such circumstances, I never like being out alone. I don't know what it is about human companionship but if I have someone with me, even if it is only Tabs, I feel much more at ease though I realise this is illogical since Tabs couldn't do anything to help if we did run into any trouble. When the lions came within two feet of the thin sheet of glass that divided us, I decided to drive off.

I had proved that the tapes worked and I didn't want *these* lions to establish a relationship with the Land Rover and associate it with food, and this they might well do if I went on playing the lion and hyena tapes. After all it was Temba and Tombi I was looking for.

Then, just as I was about to leave, the lions lay down in the middle of the road, Phuma standing out among them very clearly and a lovely sight. I had to wait a bit, until it was half past six and the lioness moved off and the cubs followed her. It had been dark for an hour so it seemed they were now about to start the night's hunt. They were moving towards Tongue Plain and this was annoying because that was where Tabby and Dimples were doing their hunting.

There seemed to be lions everywhere. The cubs were playing and jumping on top of each other and there was a lot of greeting going on, cheek rubbing, affectionate nudges and friendly bites. Phuma was the last to go. She arched her back as she followed the others along the road. In the headlights she looked snow-white. They went along the road as they usually do if it happens to go in the right direction.

I followed very slowly. Suddenly, one of the Musketeers appeared, sniffing his way along the road trying to find the others. Obviously he had overslept.

It is very difficult to observe the Machaton lions actually making a kill. For one thing, they always hunt at night, and secondly you can't follow them through thick bush country. If you do, you crash against trees and scrape the side of your vehicle and make a hell of a lot of noise which, while it doesn't seem to bother the lions, affects the prey they are stalking and makes it impossible for them to hunt effectively. Schaller managed to observe the Serengeti lions making kills at night, but that was in an area of open grass plains where he could stay well back and make relatively little noise. On bright moonlit nights, on the open grass plains, you don't even have to use the headlamps and you can follow them in a vehicle without disturbing their prey.

This explains why, although I have seen the Machaton lions on literally hundreds of kills and have often heard them make a kill, I have never seen them in the process of bringing down one of their prey animals.

When dawn broke, I was sitting by the fire in Mandaban's *guma*

We lived in the bush and
on its products:

I made biltong from strips of game

Mandabane Hlongo dried
caterpillars, a great local delicacy

A giraffe, taking a rest. You don't often see, or get a chance to photograph giraffes sitting down

Two of the vehicles we used in looking for the lions:
the old jeep, with Tabs directing operations
the plane we hired to make an air search, with Tabs in the foreground waving us off

Keith Joubert, the best wildlife artist I know, who looked after the lions
in my absence

More of our neighbours in the Bushveldt:
Zebra

White rhino

Wildebeest – their staple diet is grass and they, in turn, are number one on the lions' list of their favourite foods

Among our other neighbours in Timbavati:
Greater kudu at one of the dams

a steenbuck with ears erect, obviously disturbed and about to bolt

Buffalo coming out of the thick riverine bush onto the plains (a reed enclosure open to the sky). He had just shown me the site of another wildebeest kill, about a mile and a half from the Machaton, almost certainly made by Tabby and Dimples. Normally, Tabby and her cubs would have taken their rest beside the kill, but it seemed as though they had been excluded from any prolonged use of that area by the main sub-group. Even if I didn't know where they were resting, it was encouraging to be sure they had had a good meal.

When I got back to the lodge, Charlotte told me that our successors had been approved and appointed, and were moving in on 17 May. This meant that we would have to clear out quickly. We had been in touch with an African builder who was willing to make our mud hut and enclosure. However, until they were ready I decided to buy some tents and all the other equipment we would need for living in the bush. We also acquired some old forty-four-gallon drums for water and an old tin tub, which we'd pull up near the fire on bath night. In the rainy season we would use the river.

Our camp would have one huge advantage; it was going to be right beside Jack Mathebula's *kraal*. He is an extraordinary man, who works largely by instinct. Of course, he tracks in the ordinary way as well, from one spoor to the next, but he also has a feeling for where the lions are likely to be on any particular day, given the prevailing weather conditions. Sometimes he looks at a spoor and says, 'Now, if I were a lion in which direction would I go?' Then he examines the landscape and thinks quietly for a few seconds and finally says, 'I think I'd go that way.' And he's almost invariably right. From my point of view Jack has only one severe disadvantage: his habit of disappearing for days on end without either any warning or any explanation. I work in what I like to think of as a far more scientific way but it's also a great deal slower.

On Sunday, 15 May, I dropped in on Mandaban. He was away, but while we were there I noticed what I felt sure was a white lion spoor in the middle of his camp, in his *guma*, in fact. It was exactly the right size for the white lions. I went on to Mrs Marula's and there was spoor all over her *kraal* too. I couldn't be sure that this was made by Tabby and the white lions – it could have been the spoor of a neighbouring pride with cubs of about the same age – but it looked exactly right for Tabby and the whites.

On 17 May we moved into Nick Hancock's camp. We were to stay there until Owl Camp was a little more advanced. So far nothing had happened there and it wouldn't be safe to put up our tents without some sort of a protective stockade around them.

When I had phoned Nick and told him that we had to leave the lodge as our successors were arriving to take over from us and that Owl Camp, which was to be built on a corner of his land, was not yet in existence, he had responded magnificently, saying we could move in to his farm whenever we wanted to, and that we were to treat it as our own, using the deep freeze, fridge, beds, crockery. It was a relief because the best that we had been hoping for was permission to erect our tents inside his camp stockade, and use his water and cooking facilities. It also meant that I would be free to look full-time for the lions and, as this camp was so much closer to the part of the range Tabby and Dimples appeared to be using, we stood that much better chance of finding them.

I got Tryg's permission to shoot a giraffe. My plan was to drag it all around the area where I had seen what I thought was Tabby's spoor, chain it to a tree, play my recordings and pray that the combination of the scent left by dragging the giraffe carcass around and the sound of the hyena on a kill would be enough to attract her and the whites.

In the meantime, I found it a great pleasure to load my 'office' on to the back of the Land Rover and drive it over to Nick's. As far as packing is concerned, this has always been a very simple business for us. It consists of spreading a few blankets on the ground, throwing our possessions on to them (and, as neither of us places much stock on personal possessions, the load is usually pretty light), pull the four corners of the blankets together, load the bundles on to the back of a Land Rover or pick–up truck and get going. No carpets and underlays to be removed, no valuable silver or china to be wrapped and packed, no expensive hi–fi or TV equipment to be cossetted, not even a library of books to be transplanted. But here I should add that I do read a great deal, but my reading consists either of Shakespeare or books borrowed from libraries.

Nick Hancock's camp is in one of the most unspoilt parts of Timbavati, a landscape which has remained virtually unchanged in twenty million years, and here I felt a sense of reality that I can never find in built-up areas, much less big cities.

Most people seem to feel the same way about the low veldt. They come down here and get this bush fever (it's surprising how quickly some people catch it) and tell me, when they are leaving, how much they will miss the place. I think probably what attracts them instantly, and the nostalgia they feel when they have to leave, may be due to some of the genes that we all carry around within us, some racial memory deep within our subconscious minds. For this may be one of the cradles of the human race; only about a hundred miles from Timbavati is the site of one of the first Australopithecan finds, and many Stone Age tools and implements have been discovered in the Machaton range. Australopithecus, the Southern Ape, was one of the earliest of the man-like creatures. So, in coming to Timbavati, as far as our evolutionary background is concerned, we are only going home.

If people who have spent only a few days or weeks here feel this attraction so strongly, it is not difficult to imagine how I feel, for I walked in the veldt with my father when I was a boy of five or six; therefore this landscape has been in my genes subconsciously for millions of years, and consciously for over thirty.

CHAPTER 8

Baiting the Lions

On 18 May I started my programme of baiting the lions by shooting an impala for them. I couldn't find a suitable giraffe, by which I mean an old bull, one well past the breeding age and no longer capable of playing any effective role in the giraffe community. I had come across one possible victim just outside Nick's camp, but this was a fair distance from where I would have to drag it, and giraffes are extremely heavy to tow. It would also have meant dragging it through a portion of the range sometimes used by Phuma's sub-group and I didn't want to do that, because it might have the effect of attracting that group to the feeding station I had hoped to develop for Tabby's cubs.

I would have been happier if I'd had somebody with me when I had to leave the Land Rover to get the impala, because I had just heard what could have been a nearby lion.

It was that eerie time of the evening when the lions start to move about, so if I had happened to run into the three almost fully grown males, five lionesses and several cubs, I might have been in trouble. I was glad to get back in the Land Rover. Normally lions lie about looking as lazy and as harmless as kittens, but around sunset, they suddenly get very confident and aggressive and seem to lose a lot of their natural fear of humans. Also, I had noticed that when there are four or more people, the lions seem far more nervous than if there are only two or three. Therefore, after sundown, you are very vulnerable; ideally you should never walk in the bush after nightfall, or indeed at any time, without a companion, or a rifle – one of you to keep an eye out for lions and the other to carry a rifle capable of stopping a lion in its tracks.

In the event, I got back into the Land Rover safely, drove it to where the impala lay, put a rope around the animal's neck, tied it on to the back bumper of the vehicle and towed the carcass around, leaving a scent trail which I hoped the lions would pick up.

The impala I shot came out of the quota of five hundred which had been agreed as the minimum number that would have to be culled on the Timbavati Reserve in 1977 in order to keep the herds down to a size that the terrain could support. For that matter the reserve also had more giraffe than it could support, so some of them, too, would have to be shot.

We had heard rumours, from a very reliable source, that in certain parts of Africa not very far from us, the armies of some of the new African republics had been shooting game with machine guns to feed their people, because their countries had run out of meat. Since the departure of the whites cattle-farming had become so inefficient that it now proved necessary to call out the military with their machine guns to provide protein for the populace. If this were happening, the wildlife would be gravely endangered for they are defenceless against rifles. Any large-scale attempt to harvest them with machine guns would wipe them out just as surely as the North American bison was wiped out by the guns of the cowboys and the Indians.

The evolutionary aspect of this is that progress in the world of wildlife has not kept pace with man's and the animals have not yet had enough time to adjust itself to man's new weapons.

The flight distances of all the various species have evolved gradually over the centuries. The animals have learnt from experience how close they can allow a predator to approach before they need to start running, and this has become an instinctive reaction. An impala, for example, starts to run when it sees a cheetah at quite a considerable distance, long before it would begin to run if it saw a lion. This is because it knows instinctively that cheetah are not only a great deal faster than lions, but also have far greater staying power. If an impala sees a lion a hundred yards away, it is not much worried; it knows that it possesses the necessary speed to escape. But if it sees a cheetah half a mile away, it starts to run without a moment's hesitation.

Where man is concerned, the flight distance of an impala is attuned to the average performance of a man with a spear. Normally, impala start to run when a man approaches closer than around the maximum distance at which a good spearsman can make a kill. To an impala, man is still man the spear-carrier; and most other species of wildlife are equally far behind in their reaction to man the hunter.

I dragged the impala to Mandaban's *guma* and asked him where he thought we ought to stake it down. He suggested a dam not far away from his place, and I started to butcher the animal. Normally, the first bits that we whites eat are the liver and the kidneys, which are delicious. The Africans begin by eating the small intestines, which they roast on coals; these, too, are excellent and are a great favourite with the lions who always go for them first. The liver I proposed to fry for my breakfast the following morning. It can also be roasted over the coals and is very good done that way. Indeed, if you haven't any salt, that is the only way to cook it, because the ash from the hardwood which is used as fuel in these parts contains a certain amount of sodium chloride and other salts. This is one of the reasons why Africans always prepare it in this fashion, for salt is often scarce in Africa. Indeed, in pre-colonial days it was often used as a trading currency.

We set off in the Land Rover, dragging the remains of the impala down to the Mopani River, making as wide a scent trail as possible. Passing my uncle's camp, I saw a herd of wildebeest sleeping on the wide open swathe of land that he had cleared of all bush so that he could see the Drakensburgs. Wildebeest always choose a wide open space for sleeping. I am sure they do this as a protection against predators, so that they can see anything moving a long distance away.

We dragged the impala carcass to a tree stump and tied it. This was to be our first experimental feeding station. I then moved the Land Rover about twenty yards away, keeping the bait in the beam of my headlights, and started to play the hyena tapes. I was ready to chase away any hyena or jackal that turned up – as I was sure they would because they are highly attuned to the technique of scavenging, and have a far more efficient radar system for locating dead animals than lions have. Indeed, lions are notoriously inefficient at this, though they will usually come running to the sounds of hyena on a kill because there's nothing they like better than a meal that they haven't even had to work for.

My big worry was that I might drop asleep and that the hyenas would steal the impala before I awoke. And if the lions didn't come that night, I wanted to have enough impala left to repeat the experiment the following night.

In the event, I kept dozing off and on waking found jackals at the impala. At first I was able to scare them away by flashing the headlamps at them, but before long they became conditioned to the lights and ignored them. They were soon joined by a couple of hyena, so I decided to drag the impala another half a mile away, to Tongue Plain, where I knew Tabby and Dimples did most of their hunting.

I was beginning to feel despondent about ever finding them again, though Charlotte, like Jack, was still convinced that they were safe. At this time she was staying at the lodge for a few days in order to help our successors to take over, but I was very keen to get Jack and her out with me and put their instinctive earth feelings to work on the problem of locating the lions.* Sceptical as I am about this type of gift, I have known so many instances in the past in which their mysterious earth feelings proved uncannily accurate that I now believed them to be almost infallible.

One instance, in particular, had impressed me deeply. During our honeymoon, we were driving along the coast to what used to be Lourenço Marques. It was a really rugged road through a very wild area that was crawling with wildlife of all kinds. We arrived in a seedy little Portuguese village, miles from anywhere, a very broken-down place, oozing with character. I wanted to stop the night there because there was so much wildlife around but Charlotte suddenly said, 'I have a feeling. We should get out of here fast. I can't

---

*Charlotte possessed the same instinct as Jack, though not to the same degree.

explain why, I just know that we ought to get out of here as quickly as possible.' So on we drove for about fifty miles to another village. A few days later we read in the newspapers that all the whites in the village I had wanted to stay in had been wiped out on that night. A few hundred years ago she would have been hanged as a witch.

After that incident, despite all my doubts about extrasensory perception, I began to rely more and more on this instinct to help me to locate the lions. They found them for me again and again, and always by this curious instinct of theirs. Their announcement that something dreadful had happened to Agamemnon also proved correct – we never saw him again. They were equally convinced that Temba and Tombi were safe and well, and that we would find them before long. This was comforting.

At twenty past three I awoke to hear a lion roaring about two and a half miles away. I switched on the tape recorder, but I don't think the sound carried far enough; at any rate it produced no results. I then turned on the flashlight, which was still tied to the back of the vehicle, and saw a hyena tugging at the head of the impala. I wanted to keep intact as much of the impala as possible in case the lions should arrive, so I hooted the horn, and the hyena dashed off but within a few minutes it was back tugging at the impala carcass and quite impervious to the presence of the vehicle. I tried the hooter again, but this time he paid not the slightest attention to it. I then switched to another tape; this one was a hyena mating call. Immediately he started to lope around, pricking up his ears, no doubt wondering where this enticing sound was coming from. By now he had lost interest in the impala and was seething with passion, which I hoped was doomed to remain unfulfilled that night. I reckoned that would serve him right for trying to eat the white lions' dinner.

At four o'clock in the morning I heard the lions roaring again and felt certain that if I'd had a proper amplifier they would have come trotting up but the machine I was using wasn't nearly powerful enough. So I drove in the direction the roars seemed to be coming from – down by the Mayembule – towing the impala after me.

I remained there until dawn, but nothing showed up. Another wasted night.

By the following night there wasn't much of the impala left for the lions to feed on so I went out to shoot either an impala, or better still, a giraffe. On my way I ran into lions, though not the right ones. They were at Elephant Valley Dam, too far away to identify them. As I approached very slowly I was able to see them lying around. But there was no sign of the whites. Eventually, I spotted Phuma and also the Interloper and the Musketeers. The latter looked very thin and for a moment I wondered whether I should not feed them too, but then reflected that this would be interfering with nature and, besides, I didn't want to condition them to associating the Land Rover with food.

That evening I heard that a cameraman, Mike Dodds, was being sent out from London to collect material for a scientific documentary film on the white lions. This news made it all the more imperative to find Temba and Tombi quickly.

By now Charlotte had joined me at Nick's camp. On the way she had passed right through a pride of lions. She had no idea which pride it was, but it didn't include any whites, of that she was certain. She had had to drive through the pride pretty quickly, as she was in an open truck with Tabs in the front with her and Lucas, one of the people who was then working for us, in the back. He is afraid of lions and was terrified. He told me he thought he was going to be eaten so he just lay in the open back of the truck and closed his eyes.

A few minutes later Jack came running in to say that there were lions all around the place, only a few yards outside the perimeter of the camp. I got into the Land Rover and went after them but they scattered before I had time to identify them.

Jack and I then carved up an old bull giraffe I had shot earlier in the day and dragged sections of it all around the black soil plains, playing the tapes from time to time. Once again, we ran into Phuma's sub-group and some of them even chased the Land Rover for some distance. This was the very thing I didn't want to happen.

There was no sign of Tabby and her sub-group, which made me think that they had now developed a fear of motor cars. I knew that Bruce had been down here and he is the type of man who would be quite capable of driving up to the lions at top speed and leaping out to have a closer look at them. That was only a guess but certainly they ran away from the Land Rover on the morning that Pamela Bowling and Charlotte found Mandaban standing beside their wildebeest kill and tried to track them. On the other hand perhaps Mrs Marula had chased them off the kill and stolen some of their meat.

I was delighted that Jack had returned. Apart from being the best tracker I have ever encountered, he is a very good friend to have around. For one thing he can always sense when events are not going well for me, and can be very sympathetic in an unobtrusive way. I've found that many Africans have this capacity. They have a word for it in their own language, *ubuntu*, which means humanity. It's rather pleasant to be with someone with a genuine sense of values.

I was now able to consult two experts, Jack and Mandaban, who knew more about these lions than anybody else, one reason, of course, being that they had lived here most of the time.

Jack, in particular, knew these lions inside out. I discussed with him whether I should leave the giraffe where I had eventually staked it out near the Machaton or whether I should go out to it. He thought I should go out to it. Why? Because, if I did, I might see the two whites. I also asked him if he thought the hyenas would finish off the giraffe. 'No', he said, 'because the skin is so thick that they won't be able to bite through it.' Finally I asked him what to do if the white lions didn't come to the giraffe. He suggested dragging it to an adjoining farm. I asked if he thought we would ever find the whites. He replied, 'Perhaps'. Though he was more convinced than I was that they were still around, he wasn't prepared to be dogmatic about it. He knows Africa too well to be dogmatic about anything.

When I asked him how he had come to learn so much about lions, he told me that as a child he had spent all his time in the bush herding cattle for an old farmer called Battenhausen, and whenever a lion attacked one of the beasts, which was pretty often, he had to track it down by following the spoor. Battenhausen would then go out and shoot the lion. Sometimes, however, he only wounded them and then Jack's task was to track them down and finish them off – an occupation which instilled in him a healthy respect for lions. But he wasn't afraid of them any more than an experienced sailor is afraid of the ocean; he always treated them with respect and never took unnecessary chances, any more than a good sailor takes chances with the sea.

The next day I went with Jack and Mandaban to the place where I had left the giraffe. There were vultures sitting in a tree some four hundred yards away. This was a good sign because if there had not been lions on the carcass the vultures would have been down on top of the kill, eating.

When we reached the giraffe we could see that lions had been there – there was fresh spoor all around, probably that of Phuma's sub-group. This seemed curious because there was a shingayi tree there, ideal for resting under, but beneath its shade there was only a single jackal even though there was plenty of meat still left. Then suddenly two of the Musketeers and the Interloper appeared. The two Musketeers had exactly the same sort of eyes as Tabby and the whites: full of curiosity but not in any way hostile, whereas the Interloper had a malevolent expression. He was now developing a huge mane and looked quite sinister.

Mandaban had some interesting news for me. He said that during the night he had heard some lions roaring and from the direction from which the sound had come it couldn't have been these lions, so it was almost certainly Tabby's sub-group. He took us to the place where he thought the roars were coming from and there was plenty of fresh spoor there too. We were all convinced that this was the spoor of Tabby and her cubs. Mandaban believed they had not gone to the giraffe because by now they were frightened of the main sub-group; this was also likely to be the reason why they no longer went to the Machaton or the Mayembule. Instead they were probably hiding in the thick bush along the Maponi.

If Mandaban's theory were right, it would explain a lot of things, for while we were trying to work out whether they were afraid of cars or of humans, their problem was in fact a different one: they were afraid of *other lions* and that was why they had been forced to the very fringe of their territory. It is a well known feature of animal behaviour (Konrad Lorenz in his study of sticklebacks was one of the first to observe it and it is applicable to most species) that the further away from the centre of its territory an animal is forced to move, the more confidence it loses.

We were now convinced that Tabby and her cubs were hiding because they were afraid of other lions – not only the sub-group, but also the adjoining prides. As a result they had become peripheral members of the pride. The next stage might be nomadism, and this would almost certainly prove fatal. Indeed, unless we could keep them here, by artificial feeding, we were likely to lose them.

However tedious it might be, we now had no alternative: we must go on killing for them, dragging the carcases around the area and playing tapes, until eventually we succeeded in enticing them out of the undergrowth to sample our wares.

Once they appeared, and discovered that we were prepared to supply them with free food, I was convinced they would come regularly to the feeding station. By this means we could keep them alive and inside the Reserve until a decision was reached about their ultimate fate.

CHAPTER 9

An Idea is Born

One sleepless night I hit on what seemed to me at the time a brilliant idea, though on mature reflection it appeared to be rather mad and probably the result of lack of sleep.

I decided that when I found the lions I would hijack them, dart them, load them into the Land Rover and carry them out of the Reserve. A friend had recently applied for a permit to keep two lions, so I was going to take them to his place, spray them to look like normal lions and keep them there until I could move them from South Africa to some European zoo with a good reputation for breeding lions. I thought I would use a hired Dakota, bring it in on a nearby landing strip, dart them again and put them into the cargo compartment. We would have to organise refuelling stops for the whole journey but that would pose no special problems. I would need to persuade a vet to come with me to keep the lions sedated during the flight and make sure that they were all right.

Once they were safely in the zoo, a programme of breeding experiments could begin, so eventually a strain of white lions would be available for the world's zoos. Today many people are hostile to zoos. I think that there are some species of animals which suffer very badly from boredom when caged, but lions in my experience have always taken very kindly to captivity. Provided that the enclosure is big enough, they seem only too happy to have a regular supply of food brought to them without the bother of hunting for it.

In the case of Temba there was, I believed, no alternative. Whatever happened to Tombi, Temba was certain to be thrown out by the pride, and without camouflage, he was equally certain to die. I had watched these lions so often by night; in the moonlight, even at fifty yards, they stand out like beacons, and as a lion must get pretty close to its prey to make a successful kill, he would starve within a fortnight.

I was naturally very anxious because I feared the Timbavati Reserve Committee might defer making a decision on what to do about the white lions until it was too late.

In the meantime, I still had to find them.

The next day Mandaban and I went out tracking them; he sat up on the front of the car, so as not to frighten the lions if we came across them. In this position his outline was blurred and he would appear to be a part of the vehicle; also his scent would be smothered by the fumes from the car. From time to time, he got down to search for their spoor.

We got on to it before long, but the lions had been hunting and, when they hunt, the spoor goes all over the place.

After a couple of hours spent in losing the spoor and finding it again, we heard hyenas cackling on a kill and went to investigate. It was a fresh wildebeest kill; all that was left, in fact was a portion of the tail. I asked Mandaban what he thought had happened. There was a lot of hyena spoor all around, but also a great deal of lion spoor. He thought that the wildebeest had almost certainly been killed and eaten by Tabby and her cubs; the hyenas had then come along and taken away the bones. He reckoned that the lions might now be drinking at the nearest water hole, or resting somewhere nearby.

When we examined the spoor, we noticed that it was right over the drag marks I had made the previous day by towing the giraffe. The fact that the lions had ignored the scent from the drag might have been because they had already made the wildebeest kill and were not interested in the prospect of further food, or because they were too scared of the main sub-group to risk following the drag marks.

We spent another hour searching for them without success; probably they were resting up in the thick bush where they are almost impossible to find.

I planned to drag some meat up to Tongue Plain that evening, but as I had no clearance to shoot another giraffe, I decided to slice a leg off the one we had staked down near the Machaton, and drag it to Tongue Plain. We drove to where we had left the bait and there we met the Musketeers.

I managed to get the Land Rover between them and the carcass. The Interloper didn't seem to be around that day. What we needed to do was to slice off a leg from the bait without drawing the lions' attention to what we were doing. Jack volunteered to slip out and do the job as quickly as possible while I remained in the car with the engine running and the rifle at the ready in case there was trouble. If he was successful we would take the bait to where we believed the white lions were – somewhere near the new wildebeest kill – then drag it around a bit and finally go on to Tongue Plain and wait there, playing hyena tapes. It would of course have been easier to shoot another giraffe but I did not want to break the rules.

Jack crept round the other side of the Land Rover from the lions. They were about thirty-five yards away. Since the car was between them and the carcass I reckoned he would be safe enough. I spent my time trying to keep one eye on Jack and another on the lions, making sure that he had not disturbed them. In fact they were fast asleep but as he sharpened his knife one of the lions woke up and looked around, on hearing the noise. However, as he couldn't see Jack, he seemed to assume that it came from the Land Rover and dropped off to sleep again.

After using a knife Jack was obliged to take an axe to sever the bone. When this had been accomplished he came back to me and gave me the knife. Then he took the chain out very quietly through the bars of the cage around the Land Rover, and hooked it on to the leg. But he was not able to go around to the back of the vehicle to fasten the chain there because if he had done so the lions would certainly have seen him. Instead he fastened it along the side farthest from the lions and there it would have to remain until we got well away from the area. Obviously, it would scratch the paintwork but we would have to put up with that.

Having accomplished his task, he got back into the Land Rover and we moved away. The lions could not see that we were dragging the bait because it was on the far side of the car from them, but one of the Musketeers was wide awake and took far too much interest in our activities for my liking.

Jack carried out the whole operation magnificently. I asked him if he wasn't afraid and he replied, 'No, I wasn't afraid, because I have a strong heart, but I'm planning to get a bit further away from them before I transfer the leg to the back.'

When we had done this, we took the leg to where we believed the white lions were hiding, dragged it around the place, and then tied it to a tree. I planned to return at night and try out the hyena tapes.

While I was sitting there alone, playing the lion and hyena tapes, it occurred to me that though I must use them until I had succeeded in attracting the lions to the vehicle and until I had conditioned them to the idea that the vehicle meant free food, after that there would be no need to continue playing those ghastly cacklings and roars. Pavlov conditioned his dogs to come to the sound of a bell, so any sound would do once I had managed to get it firmly associated in the minds of the animals with the notion of food.

I would have to continue to use the hyena tapes until I had succeeded in finding and feeding the lions, but later I would switch to music, playing it very gently at first and then gradually increasing the volume. Because I like Beethoven, I decided to start with his Violin Concerto, or the Triple Concerto.

This would not only relieve me of the tedium of listening to the hyena tapes, it would also be *selective*. Any of these lions would have come to the sound of hyenas on a kill; but only the white lions would come to Beethoven, because they alone would associate Beethoven with food. This would mean that I wouldn't waste valuable time (and meat) attracting the wrong lions, and when the time came for darting the whites, it would avoid having to cope with the possible presence of other lions. This was very important for, if the main sub-group showed up on the night we planned to dart the whites, it might mean postponing the whole business, as there was a danger that the whites might be attacked by the others while still under the effect of the drugs and unable to defend themselves. Also it would be unsafe for us to get out of the vehicles and load the white lions on to a truck without darting or shooting every lion in sight – an almost impossible task.

Although the lions didn't come that night, I felt that it hadn't been wasted, for I had hit on an idea that was going to simplify the whole business of darting the whites when the time came.

By now, we were living in Nick Hancock's camp on the northeast of the Reserve, near the Kruger Park fence; a very simple camp, built on the principle that if anything went wrong you couldn't get repair men and so had to do everything yourself, and if you needed spare parts you might have to drive hundreds of miles, so why bother? Nick saw no point in trying to run a luxury camp because he knew, from experience, that many of the owners who tried to do so spent so much of their time fixing up the numerous things that went wrong that they hadn't any time left to spend in the bush, which was the whole point of having a camp.

He had only an old paraffin fridge that worked once in a while, a small gas deep freeze (the height of luxury) and, for sanitation, a long drop, with a reed screen around it and a thatched roof. He had unbreakable metal cups and plates and three-legged pots for making stew. The bedrooms were thatched *rondavels*, round with conical roofs, based on the traditional African pattern. There was a primitive bathroom, consisting of an ancient shower fed from a forty-four-gallon drum outside, under which you had to light a wood fire if you wanted hot water. It is a bit more complicated than simply turning on a tap, but it worked. He had also built a big *guma*, a reed enclosure, for eating out of doors on windy days, and another thatched structure, without any walls, to act as a lounge.

On Thursday 19 May, Peter Dickson, a scriptwriter from Hollywood, arrived to write a screenplay for a feature film based on *The White Lions of Timbavati*. I took him to the giraffe carcass to show him some lions, but the Musketeers had temporarily deserted it.

That evening Charlotte saw two lionesses, one lactating and the other heavily pregnant. They were pride lionesses from the Velvet Paws pride, of which Achilles now appeared to be in sole command. Charlotte thought that if the lionesses were pregnant from Achilles, which seemed very likely, and that if he were Agamemnon's brother, as we both believed him to be, then there was a strong possibility of white lions being born into the Velvet Paws pride.

During her drive Charlotte had visited Lena, Mrs Marula's daughter, and had named her new baby Roseanne. Roseanne was dedicated to Charlotte. It is a local tribal tradition to dedicate a child to some famous or wealthy man or woman thereby hoping to ensure some security for its future. In Roseanne's case, this meant that Charlotte would get medicine for her every time she fell sick and generally act as district nurse.

Mrs Marula is every bit as formidable in her dealings with mankind as she is in regard to the lions. She was originally married to Moskin, who was then looking after my father's camp, and she bore him a number of children. Apart from Lena, the only one living with her in the bush, there were five, all then working in the big cities; and Zandy, Jack's wife, who lived near the site of Owl Camp.

You could describe Mrs Marula as the first woman's libber to live in the bush. When, a few years earlier, Moskin had taken a second wife, a very pretty little fifteen-year-old, which he was perfectly entitled to do under the local tribal laws, Mrs Moskin, as she then was, issued an edict: either Moskin threw out the young lady at once, or she would leave him. This was most unusual behaviour for not only is it legal for a Shangaan to take a second wife (or indeed as many young wives as he fancies) it is also a custom widely accepted as a normal way of life.

Moskin replied that the young lady in question was his *impahala* (which literally means baggage, an indication of the way in which women are thought of and treated in the bush), so it was none of Mrs Moskin's business.

Without further discussion she walked out, taking the children with her. She moved a few miles away, changed her name to Mrs Marula and established a *kraal* of her own where she lived with Lena and an assortment of grandchildren born to her sons and daughters who from time to time sent money from the city as well as sending her their offspring.

Before long, Moskin's young 'baggage' deserted him for someone younger and more attractive, so he was left alone and, as he remarked, 'like an old wildebeest', thrown out of the herd. He seemed, in fact, to be happy, and congratulating himself on not having a crowd of women around the place chattering and making a noise. Despite their 'divorce', Mrs Marula still looked after him whenever he fell sick and was always bringing him food and sending the children over to see how he was doing.

On Tuesday 23 May Charlotte and Jack went out in the Land Rover while I went out in a hired Land Rover with Peter Dickson.

Charlotte took Tabs, Robert and the African children with her and before long they came across some lion spoor – it appeared to be the fresh spoor of two cubs and a lioness.

Jack took his gun and went into the bush to follow the paw marks but it was a very windy day and he wasn't too hopeful of being able to find the lions. When, after about two hours, there was no sign of them, Charlotte drove back to camp. On the way there they saw more lion spoor, but it was getting too late to track it. Meanwhile, Jack followed the lions for miles without any success until late in the evening, when he had realised that Charlotte must have returned to the camp with the children, and walked all the way home.

He told us he had followed the spoor till he found a place where the lions had been sleeping in the thick bush. After this he followed their trail down again to Tongue Plain, where the grass is very high. Spooring lions through the long grass is a very tedious, dangerous business and to have followed them any further into thick bush would have been suicidal, all the more so because Jack was on his own and there was only one bullet in the gun.

On our trip, Dickson and I had seen a lion's head sticking out over the wall at Park Dam, but it disappeared almost immediately. The animal was obviously very nervous of the car which was unusual for a Machaton lion. We followed the spoor slowly and spotted some lions, but they were very wary and moved away from the Land Rover. This again was very unusual and indicated to me that they had been subjected to some sort of disturbance, possibly from the new and inexperienced safari camp operators who had replaced us. We sat tight for about forty minutes, after which the lions began to emerge but were still very wary. We drove slowly around the thicket, and came upon a beautiful sleek lioness, lying in the sun. Further on some cubs came out and started to play around the Land Rover apparently no longer afraid of it. They were from Phuma's sub-group, but we saw no sign of her. About an hour and a half before dark we returned, leaving the lions still in the thicket. Three, four, five cubs came right up to the Land Rover, so close in fact that I had to put the window up. I took a picture from less than three feet away, and one of the cubs actually sneezed right into the lens. We waited until the sun went down, but still there was no sign of Phuma. So, though Peter had seen his first lions in the wild, he hadn't yet seen a white one.

CHAPTER 10

A Night to Remember

We went on searching day after day and night after night but had seen no sign of Temba and Tombi for almost exactly two months. Then Jack suddenly announced that he had a feeling we were going to find the lions that very night, 29 May, on a dam near the very south-western fringe of the range. Earlier he had been out with Peter, and they had found a buffalo kill, the first in that area so far as we knew, in almost two years and he was convinced it had been made by Tabby, Dimples and the whites and that if we returned in the evening they would still be there.

I had now reached a decision of some importance: not to play any more tapes of lions on a kill. For it had struck me that if it was the other sub-group of which Tabby and her cubs were nervous, then there was no way that they would emerge from the thick bush to the sound of lions on a kill. From now on it had better be undiluted hyena tapes at least until I had started to feed them and initiated my plan of conditioning them to dining out to the strains of Ludwig Van.

On the way to the dam where Jack predicted we would find the lions, we stopped off at Tongue Plain to pick up the back legs I had staked down there the previous night. I was intending to use them to pin the lions to the spot while we went away and shot an impala for them.

However, when we got there, all the meat was gone, eaten to the bone by the hyenas; stupidly, as it turned out, we hadn't loaded any other meat into the Land Rover. So if Jack proved to be right and we did find the white lions, we now had nothing with which to feed them.

We drove right across Tongue Plain to the very south-western fringe of the territory – in fact I wasn't sure at the time that we didn't go beyond the extreme fringe of their range. We did, in fact, as I discovered later from my maps. And there we found the cubs, hale and hearty and as snow-white as ever.

I saw Tabby first and one of the white cubs, then the second white came right up to the car, and finally Dimples arrived, greeted Tabby and lay down quite unconcerned by our presence.

It was very annoying that we had no meat because that would have pinned the lions down to the place.

I saw that the white cubs were now as big as their mother, though Vela, the brown one, was a little smaller. They looked very fit.

I told Jack how relieved I was to have found them to which he replied firmly that he, for his part, had never had the smallest doubt. Vela came so close that I could hear his feet scratching the grass. Then he sat down on his haunches less than five feet from our right-hand window while Temba lay about eight paces to the rear.

Around half past twelve Tabby was on the move and I thought that the night hunt was going to begin. The question then arose: should we follow them, even if it meant wrecking their hunt? More-over, if they went through thick bush it would be impossible for us to keep up with them. All the same I was for having a try since, if we could remain with them until dawn when they would rest, we would then know where to find them later on when we could bring some meat for them. We decided to take a chance on it and follow them.

It proved to be awful bush to take a Land Rover through but we decided to stick to them even if it meant ruining their hunt.

After a while Dimples turned back to see what we were up to. She and the Interloper are the two most menacing lions I have ever encountered and even Jack was wary of them. Tabby came back too. She was a beautiful lioness and no one was ever frightened of her. It was obvious that now they were hunting seriously – perhaps they could smell the remains of the giraffe.

About half an hour later Charlotte had the idea of throwing the mattress out of the window for them to play with. She thought it might keep them in one place for a time. Almost immediately they ripped it to pieces and set off again. We followed them to an area that was unfamiliar to us so we took the precaution of leaving a trail of mealie meal that we had in the back of the Land Rover thinking that, thanks to it, we would be able to find our way back. Meanwhile we concentrated on trying to keep the lions in sight.

Around half-past one we kept coming up to big humps that looked like boulders but were in fact bits of the mattress that the lions had pulled to pieces in the space of five minutes. They were now definitely hunting seriously but this the cubs combined with romping and playing amongst themselves, and Vela still with a piece of mattress in his mouth.

At about 5 a.m. there were some anxious moments when we lost the pride in thick bush, not indeed that we had any idea where we were. Then they reappeared. The Land Rover was getting horribly scratched but I felt it was worth while following the lions regardless.

I realised that if it hadn't been for the whites we should have lost them very quickly but we were able to see Temba and Tombi at a distance of fifty yards when the two lionesses and Vela were completely invisible. This convinced me that the whites would never be able to make a kill.

In spite of their being so conspicuous we did in fact lose the pride at half-hourly intervals. Then I would play the hyena tapes and invariably they came back.

All through the night we went on driving, buoyed up by the fact that once the sun had risen, the lions would settle down to sleep and then, after marking the spot, we could go away. Later, I would shoot something for them and in the evening we would return and I would start conditioning them to Beethoven. Meanwhile it was a long exhausting grind. By six o'clock I was in such thick bush that I was terrified I might run over one of the lions. Already Dimples had come back once and had crouched down in front of the Land Rover threatening us. When she moved off I followed the pride and reflected that the lions moving through the bush in single file without making a sound were a menacing sight. The two lionesses were leading and the cubs trailing after them. Obviously the poor things were hungry but of course they had no chance of making a kill with the Land Rover clumping behind and tearing off branches as it advanced. The noise of the engine did not in fact bother the lions but it must have scared all game away for miles around.

After losing them again I caught up with the cubs sniffing at the ground. They set off in single file like a string of beads. I realised that the lionesses must be ahead and out of sight and the cubs were trying to trace them by scent.

I now recognised the place and realised that we were close to a little river that runs – whenever it does – south-west of my father's camp. We bumped along and at intervals there were frightful crashes as we bounced over rocks and I could only hope that we had not fractured the sump. Finally, we realised that the lionesses had totally disappeared.

All the others in the Land Rover were fast asleep, but I drove on in the direction I thought the lions were heading. As we went over yet another rock the tape recorder fell off the roof and was smashed. After that I had no way of calling the lions back; the little recorder on which I was making notes of the night's events was not nearly powerful enough.

I drove on until I came to a road and stopped there for a bit to consider my next move. Jack woke up, and when I told him what had happened he said, 'Just drive up that road and we'll find them.' We did so, and there they were.

We followed them as they walked right along the fence around that wedge of land that juts like an arrowhead into the edge of the Timbavati Reserve. We weren't at all happy at seeing them in this part of the Reserve because of the dangerous proximity of the farm owned by the man who had boasted that he had stopped counting when he had shot two hundred lions.

We were even more apprehensive when one of the white cubs turned and tried to scramble under the fatal fence. Luckily, he didn't make it, and returned to the others who continued to walk along by the fence. Eventually Tabby turned right and we lost them. By now it was getting light and if we hadn't lost the tape recorder, we might have called them back and stuck with them until they settled down for their day's sleep.

This time, for once, Jack's instinct let him down, and although we combed the area for over an hour, we could not find any trace of them.

So the White Lions of Timbavati were lost again; but at least we now knew they were alive and well and we also knew roughly where to start looking for them again that night.

CHAPTER 11

Establishing a Routine

My own most urgent problem when we got back to camp was to get hold of some tape recording equipment and fresh hyena tapes. It was imperative to get these immediately and to go back around sunset to the area where we had last seen the lions; this time with plenty of meat.

I knew that John Dunning, a friend of mine who worked at the nearby Giraffe Camp, had a lot of very sophisticated tape recorders and amplifiers and a big collection of tapes, so I called on him and asked him to lend me some equipment for a night or two until I could replace my own. I told him what had happened and he provided me with a terrific tape recorder, an amplifier and a loud speaker which had a range of about three kilometres, as well as some beautiful new tapes of hyenas cackling on a kill. The amplifier worked off the car battery and the loudspeaker gave superb reproduction; there was no comparison between this equipment and the amateur stuff I had been using.

John also gave me some useful advice on the methods he used when playing tapes of hyena calls to attract lions. 'If you are trying to lure lions,' he said, 'you must always drag in a circle. Lions are extremely lazy and if you drag in a straight line and they pick up the trail and happen to follow it away from the bait, when they come to the end of the trail they will simply continue walking in a straight line. It would never occur to them to turn around and follow up the trail the other way. But if you drag in a circle they must eventually come to the bait, whichever way they go. It's rather like being on the Circle Line in the London Underground – even if you take a train going in the wrong direction, you will reach the right station eventually. And,' he added, 'while you are laying the trail, you should play a few hyena whoops from time to time, to get the lions interested, and lure them; with the powerful amplifier and big speaker this should pose no problems.'

We set out that evening at about half-past five, towing a giraffe leg. We made a circle around the area where we had seen the cubs on the previous night, and played the hyena tapes on John's amplifier. Within half an hour the lions came up to the Land Rover and spent the whole night with us, eating and resting and playing and then eating again, obviously completely at ease. At times one or other actually slept resting against a wheel.

Just before dawn, they disappeared. One minute they were there, the next they had gone. We didn't try to follow them because we knew now that we could find them again. The fact that they had disappeared so suddenly at the first signs of dawn confirmed my view that it was the other lions that they were avoiding. There's a stretch of very thick bush along the Maponi River; I had known lions to hide out there in the past. My guess was that this was the place Tabby had chosen to hide with her cubs.

I decided to establish a feeding station just to the west of Tongue Plain and near the Maponi, because I wanted to pin the cubs to a spot well away from the danger fence – but not so close to the Machaton range that Tabby would feel threatened by the main sub-group. But I would have to take this in easy stages.

The next night I went out on my own; Peter had had enough. I tried at first to find the cubs in the area where we had last fed them, but all I could manage to attract with the hyena tapes were other hyena. This was the last thing I wanted because they would soon make short work of the remains of the bait. So I scared them off and moved eastwards towards the northern end of Tongue Plain, dragging the giraffe leg and playing the tapes intermittently.

As I approached the Maponi the cubs came up out of the river bed and went straight to the remains of the bait, almost as if they had been expecting a meal to be served to them in that way. I also had a couple of fresh impala legs in the Land Rover, one of which I immediately threw out. Tabby got it, and carried it about three yards away before settling down to eat it. I fed some smaller joints to Vela and the white cubs.

At one stage, when they were pulling at the remains of the giraffe, I could feel the Land Rover being dragged back, which showed how strong they were, because a Land Rover weighs the best part of a ton and the brakes were on.

I decided that this spot was going to be my feeding station number one. Later, when I got the lions conditioned to being fed in this way, I might try to establish one or more alternative feeding stations still further away from the danger area. But in many ways this place was ideal. The grass had been grazed flat; it was only about an inch high which made it perfect for photography. Mike Dodds, the cameraman, was coming to stay and I realised we should have to warn him that he would need to bring lighting equipment as these lions were only appearing after dark and disappearing into the thick bush again just before dawn.

The place had one disadvantage: it was too close to Mrs Marula's *kraal* for my liking. The children there tend to wake up at all hours and start chattering and playing transistor radios. I decided to call on her and ask her to try and keep them quiet at least for the next few days; now that I had got the lions used to being fed from the vehicle I didn't want them being frightened away by the sound of human voices. And when I was ready to switch over to the conditioning process I didn't want them to hear any music apart from Beethoven.

In every other way this site was ideal. There was even a little rocky *kopje*, not more than a hundred feet high, but in this flat country that is quite an eminence and from its summit you could see – and film – the low veldt for miles around.

The fact that the spot lay to the west of the Maponi river bed made it virtually inaccessible to cars. Even in the Land Rover, it's a hell of a job to get through the river: you have to drive down one almost perpendicular river bank, then plough for at least two hundred yards through the sand of the river bed and finally struggle up the opposite side whereever there is a break in the bush. It is accessible from the west but, as there are no roads there, I didn't think anybody was likely to approach it from that direction. This would greatly reduce the possibility of visitors finding and photographing the white lions though, in any case, since they only came out after dark, and by then most of the tourists would be far more interested in pink gins than white lions, the risk was minimal.

I expected the lions to feed here happily after dark and then melt away at dawn into the thick bush. Now I could see the situation from Tabby's point of view: to the north and east lay the core area of the Machaton range, which had been expropriated by the main sub-group. And although Tabby and Dimples were members of the same pride, they had temporarily been excluded because their cubs were by then so big that they constituted a menace to the sub-group's much smaller ones. To the south, there were various other prides. The only vacuum was away to the west, beyond the fatal fence, where any lions that appeared could be shot as vermin; but Tabby couldn't know this, so if she couldn't find enough food in the Maponi area, she would inevitably tend to wander off westwards. It was quite clear to me that it was essential to feed her and her cubs regularly to prevent her from going west in search of fresh territory.

This explained many things. Obviously Tabby was only emerging from the thick bush at night, roaming around with her cubs, looking for food, but making no sound and avoiding the main sub-group as much as possible. That was why we hadn't been able to find her by listening for roars; she'd been deliberately not roaring because she had been afraid of attracting the attention of these lions. Also, there was a big nomad male lion in this area – I had seen him several times – and she wouldn't want to attract his attention either, because that might cause friction with the cubs.

It explained why they hadn't come out to me before, because then I had been playing tapes of lions on a kill as well as the hyena tapes and if it was lions that Tabby was avoiding, naturally she wouldn't come anywhere near us while we were using the lion tapes.

As the night wore on I began to feel increasingly nervous. When we were watching the lions before we started feeding them I had never felt nervous because they had ignored the vehicle; indeed they behaved as though it were invisible.

Now, because they related it to food, they were acutely aware of it. And, with only a sheet of glass between me and them, I felt distinctly uncomfortable, particularly whenever Dimples approached. She stretched, then came towards my window and the hairs on the back of my neck stood on end. Soon she was less than a yard away and was looking at me through the windscreen. I said to myself, this is what happens when you start feeding lions, they get altogether too interested in the car and this was just what I wanted to avoid.

Luckily at this point Dimples walked away. It is curious how different the two lionesses are. Tabby was a great character, very casual and never menacing. She was a good mother and a great hunter and she hadn't got the dangerous streak that her friend had.

Now meat every evening had become an accepted fact so each day I needed to shoot something. I did not enjoy doing this but it was inevitable and for that matter less horrible for the victim than being pulled down by lions.

At about half past three, the morning star rose in the east, very low and very bright. Not long afterwards a giraffe and a small jackal approached to within twenty paces of Temba but would not venture closer. Generally, jackals know what is a safe distance but they keep a very close look-out, and if the lion is momentarily distracted they will nip in and nick some of the meat. Suddenly the lioness walked past one of my headlamps; I could only see the tips of her ears but as I felt no apprehension, I was sure it must be Tabby. Temba is another lion for whom I feel no fear; in fact I am as much at ease with him as if he were a donkey.

That night, with time on my hands, I began to wonder about lions' ears – why they were black at the back. Nothing happens in nature without a reason. Then it occurred to me that since lionesses usually hunt as a team, the black on the back of their ears and on the tips of their tails is probably a form of visual communication, enabling them to keep in touch during the hunt. When stalking, lions flatten out so that they become invisible to their prey from the front,

94

since their ears are the same tawny colour as the grass. But from behind, the black tips of ears and tails would be visible and the pride members behind would know where the leading lioness was. Also the flicking of their tails could be another form of visual communication.

The beautiful fluid walk of the lions, which is such a joy to watch, must also have a purpose. One purpose is obvious: this lazy, loping gait conserves the maximum amount of energy which they need for that short, sharp burst of speed that will enable them to make a successful kill.

It may also have another purpose, though this is speculation (as indeed most observations about wild animals must be). Isn't it just possible that the movements they make fall outside the visual range of the ungulates, which are their principal prey? Maybe this is a bit 'way out' as a theory, but it may be that ungulates are only capable of observing certain types of movement, just as human ears are only capable of hearing certain sounds.

But back to that night in the bush, the first night I had spent out alone with the lions – the first of many, as it turned out.

Temba came right up to me, peering into the Land Rover's cage. All I could see were two little ears and his eyes looking directly at me. He was by then a big lion and beautiful. Soon Tabby joined him. She was being very skittish and bounded off into the bush after something. These lions are so fast and so unpredictable that if one of them ever decided to attack it would all be over in a split second – human reflexes are far too slow. It is only in the wild that you appreciate the power that lions possess. The lionesses, in particular, combine this with a high turn of speed. Male lions are not nearly as deadly as lionesses; and, with their black manes, more conspicuous. (The mane is an example of an evolutionary development connected with sex. Its purpose, like that of the tail of a peacock, is to attract.)

A little jackal was waiting. He knew where the meat was and returned hopefully but the lions wouldn't let him get to it so the poor devil went hungry. For that matter I was hungry too, as I had nothing but tea and tobacco with me. Vela lay so close to the Land Rover I could hear him breathing. Later a wildebeest snorted about half a mile away down in the plains and I wondered if he was heralding the approach of the other lions. This fear made me realise that if we were going to establish the feeding station we would need to watch out carefully for other prides. I did not want the cubs frightened nor did we wish to run a canteen for all the lions of Timbavati.

Never had I seen Tabby as playful as she was that night. When the cubs were younger she frequently played with them. I wondered what had got into her, but perhaps it was simply that the night was chilly and she was trying to keep warm.

It was five past five when I heard the first bird call. There was as yet no sign of the sun but the birds seemed to know that somehow it was not far off.

It was at about this hour the previous day that the lions melted away. Would they do so again?

When the first dim glow of dawn came, I was able to distinguish a strange lion. I thought it might have been the Interloper or possibly one of the Musketeers. If that were so, it was all right for they were still commuting between the two sub-groups, but if a strange lion was lurking about I might have to shoot him, regardless of the regulations.

It was not long before Tabby decided to move off with her family. After some indecision, they went north, the worst direction from my point of view because the area was so rocky. Nevertheless, in spite of the damage it might do to the Land Rover, I determined to stay right behind the lions but keeping my distance, for Dimples had turned around and looked me straight in the eyes as though to warn me.

As it grew lighter, I saw the party loping along Tongue Plain. Dimples again turned and gave me a long glare. I decided to keep still further behind for I did not want to annoy the old girl too much. I drove forward very slowly and saw that the lions were heading straight for the Mayembule and going there by a route which was not their normal one. Here the riverine bush was at its thickest and most inaccessible.

When I finally lost them it was ten minutes to seven. I would never have thought, had I been tracking them, to look for them where they had gone, because they had never gone there in the past. At least I had learnt not to look for them any more on any of their regular routes, or what used to be their regular routes. They were probably lying up for the day in the river bed – another thing they never do, or rather, never did.

A little duiker had just run out in front of the Land Rover. This tiny antelope, a little grey buck, about the size of a steinbok, is called a duiker because of its habit of ducking down in the tall grass. Duiker means ducker or diver.

I was very happy because I no longer had any doubts that we could find the white lions again whenever we needed to.

CHAPTER 12

The Meeting of the Lions

Around this time I started to get all sorts of letters, many of them idiotic, from people who had read about the white lions. One man seriously asked, 'Don't you think you ought to shoot these lions? Otherwise they're going to spread this useless white strain all over Africa.' He didn't realise that if a genetic aberration such as a white mutation happens to crop up among lions, there's no chance that it will spread rapidly unless that mutation happens to be of advantage to the species as a whole. Melanism – a genetic mutation which produces a black pigmentation, as opposed to leucism, which produces a white effect – proved an advantage to leopards and consequently spread rapidly with the result that black leopards are now quite common. But it can be of no advantage to a lion to be white in the bushveldt.

Other correspondents advanced the theory that as animals are colourblind, the white lions should be just as capable of hunting for themselves as any normal lions, since their prey species, being colourblind, could not see that they were white.

This is nonsense. Even assuming that animals, or some species of animals, are colourblind, or see colours in a different way from us, they still see, and the way they see is by the reflection of light from the object at which they are looking. Now a white lion, because it is white, must necessarily reflect more light and therefore be more visible to the prey animal, whether or not he is colourblind, whereas a tawny lion reflects roughly the same amount of light as

98

the dried up bushveldt in which he spends so much of his time.

I also learned that someone from the London Zoo had described the white lions on a British television programme as 'genetic freaks'. This sounds pejorative, but is true; the white lions *are* genetic freaks. For that matter a great many scientists believe that the big reasoning brain in humans is also the result of a genetic freak, a chance mutation which happened to prove useful to the species and consequently became a dominant strain and spread rapidly. This could be one explanation for the fact that man's evolution seems to have out-stripped that of all other species and at an almost lunatic speed. The lion or the impala of ten thousand years ago was not very different from the lion or the impala of today. In the same period man has progressed, if that is the word, from a spear carrier to a creature capable of leaving this planet and exploring space, a creature who has replaced his spear with nuclear weapons capable of destroying every vestige of life on earth at the press of a button.

Personally, I believe that man is a genetic freak rapidly heading towards extinction. Here is an interesting statistic which provokes thought: all species appear to have a certain lifespan after which they become extinct, and if you relate what is known about the average lifespan of various species to the human three score and ten lifespan, man is still only nine years old. The fact that he seems to be on the point of achieving his own extinction at such an early age might be the direct result of the fact that he is a genetic freak and has not evolved according to the age-old laws of nature.

Mutation is in one sense a perfectly natural process and is perhaps the only theoretical framework that can explain the extraordinary diversity of species of life found on this planet, both at the present time and in the distant past. The danger is that this one genetic freak, man, has achieved the potential to destroy the habitat for all the other species as well as his own, except perhaps for insects, which may turn out to be the sole survivors.

In the meantime, and for as long as he lasts, twentieth-century man has full control over his own environment, and he has brought about this situation as a result of his own technology. This is probably why civilised twentieth-century man finds it extremely hard to come to terms with a primitive environment in its natural state, virtually unaltered since the time of the first man-like creatures. It is an environment which is uncontrolled (except by the laws of nature) and to some extent uncontrollable. This also explains the difficulty civilised twentieth-century man has in understanding the Africans' way of thinking – their stoical acceptance of everything that happens because it is beyond their control and consequently not worth worrying about.

Around five that evening, Jack and I went out in the Land Rover. We planned to shoot an impala before the sun went down and then head for the feeding station area. In case we didn't find an impala before the sun went down, I had brought along a very strong torch: if you get an impala in the beam it is dazzled and stands there transfixed long enough for you to shoot it. This is the method we employ when culling impala, except that instead of a flashlight we use a much stronger searchlight which works off the car batteries.

As we drove along we didn't see an impala, only some kudu, but I wouldn't shoot one of them, they're too scarce.

There was a very bright moon that night, which rendered the dazzling beam from a torch far less effective. When we're culling, we always avoid moonlit nights. But, in this instance, we had no choice. We caught a cheetah in the beam, a beautiful sight, and later a roaming band of hyena which were quite unconcerned by the light; probably they were the hyena that had been around the bait during the past couple of nights and had become accustomed to the car headlamps.

Later we saw a leopard, pinned for a second in the beam, then slinking away into the bush. They are extraordinarily agile creatures; one minute you see them and the next they've disappeared without a trace and they are so rapid that you don't actually see them go.

It was half past eight before I managed to bag an impala and I used Tryg's rifle because it was too risky shooting at a four-inch target from fifty yards away at night with a .22 without telescopic sights. With the rifle, I could shoot for the shoulder, which is a much bigger area, and be sure of making a clean kill. If you shoot for the shoulder with a .22, the animal might run for quite a distance before dropping, and at night it could be difficult to find it and make sure it was dead. With a large rifle, if I hit it in the shoulder it would die instantly.

I had decided to establish a second feeding station, about half a mile from the first one, on the far side of the Maponi River and on the extreme western edge of Tongue Plain. This is because I thought that if somebody were staying in my father's camp, I could use feeding station number two, which is on the far side of the Maponi from Vlak; and if there were someone staying at my uncle Robert's camp, I could use feeding station number one, which is on the far side of the Maponi from him. Tabby's principal concern was to avoid other lions; mine was to avoid other humans. I didn't want them wandering around the feeding stations and upsetting the lions; equally I didn't want to annoy anyone staying at either camp by playing the hyena tapes and later the Beethoven music. With the equipment I was now using the racket could be heard for miles around, and visitors come down to Timbavati for peace and quiet.

As soon as we reached Tongue Plain, I began to play a hyena tape. Within ten minutes a lion had appeared. It was one of the Musketeers and he came straight along the road, missing the scent from the drag mark and heading for my Land Rover, from which the hyena sounds were coming. He appeared puzzled at not being able to find the beasts that were making so much noise, but because he had never been fed from the car, he didn't associate it with food and consequently paid no attention to us.

Soon he was joined by the other Musketeer, and then by the Interloper. By then some roaring was coming from the direction of the Mayembule: it was most likely the lionesses of Phuma's sub-group. I thought that probably these three lions were paying Tabby and her sub-group a visit, since at this stage they appeared to be still commuting between the two groups.

The Interloper roared in answer to the lionesses, a full-throated roar, a magnificent, terrifying sound. It was clear that by now these three were becoming the pride males; neither the Interloper nor the

Musketeers would have dared to roar like that while Agamemnon and Achilles were around.

There wasn't a breath of air, the night was chilly and absolutely still apart from the roaring of the lions and the other sounds of an African night.

Suddenly a white lion appeared and instinctively I threw out a piece of meat. Then I saw it was Phuma. I should have recognised her from her size. This was exactly what I didn't want to do; to condition Phuma and her sub-group to the idea that the Land Rover represented free meat.

I drove away fast, but Phuma pounded after us, hell for leather. One of the other lions, probably a Musketeer, also chased us. It was the first time that we had ever been chased by the lions but I was sure it wouldn't be the last and I surmised that some tourist was going to get a hell of a shock one of these days when instead of ignoring his jeep, as lions normally do, this pride began chasing him all over the reserve.

Eventually I shook them off and we headed back to where we had staked down the remains of the giraffe. On the way, Jack suggested that we should stop and load the impala that we were dragging into the back of the Land Rover, in case we again ran into members of the wrong sub-group.

When we got back to the giraffe we found Temba and Tombi with Vela and the two lionesses, feeding on it, though it must have been stinking by then. Immediately we fed them the impala. Although they seemed more nervous than they had been on the previous night, they soon came for the meat. Jack and I did our best to see that the two whites got their fair share; after all, they were our principal concern.

Before long we came to the end of the meat we had with us in the cab. We had to drive some distance to get the rest of the impala out of the back and drag it back to them. Jack suggested that I should turn around to face the the lions, so that they couldn't see him fiddling at the back of the vehicle. He did the job quickly and soon slipped in beside me. We were anxious to get back to the whites because the two sub-groups were only about half a mile away from one another, and there was every chance of a meeting. If that happened,

I wanted to be there to see what their various reactions would be.

We dragged the impala back, and immediately Vela grabbed it and once again started to drag the Land Rover, against the brakes. It was rather like being towed along in a boat by a big fish. Soon Temba and Tombi joined Vela on the impala carcass. Tabby just sat by placidly, watching her cubs eat. Probably she had already eaten all she needed for that night.

We saw no sign of the other sub-group, though we could hear them roaring, quite close. Vela looked up anxiously and stopped eating for a couple of minutes whenever he heard them. Neither Tabby nor Dimples roared back, as they would have done in the past. Clearly, they didn't want to give the other lions any indication of their whereabouts.

Suddenly there came a monstrous roar, probably the Interloper from the sound of it. This time the cubs all stopped eating and looked around anxiously. Tabby didn't seem unduly concerned, though she did not reply to the roar.

After a few minutes they all relaxed again and went back to the impala. Again we could feel the car being pulled backwards as they tried to tear off pieces they could take into the bush and eat in comfort.

We discussed whether to drive some distance away and cut the cord, so that the lions could eat the impala in peace, instead of tugging at the car. But when we did so, they all chased after the vehicle just as Phuma and the Musketeer had done earlier that night. At one stage we were dragging a couple of them along bodily as they clung to the carcass. They seemed to regard it as a bit of a lark.

Once again, as with Phuma and the Musketeer, we soon out-stripped them for long enough for Jack to slip out of the cab, cut the cord, and load the impala on to the Land Rover. Then we hurried back to them, and threw it out.

They were obviously still hungry and quite undisturbed by the chase for they settled down happily to finish off the carcass.

Still there was no sign of the other sub-group. Then suddenly one of the Musketeers appeared. Temba was feeding on the giraffe at the time and the Musketeer went straight for him. Temba fled.

I asked Jack how they could know that there was food there. 'Maybe a wind,' he said, in Zulu. 'The wind is in the right direction but sometimes they know in their hearts where there is food.'

The second Musketeer arrived, and all three cubs fled into the bush. Then the Interloper appeared and moved in a stalking crouch, threatening the cubs. Finally the rest of the sub-group came and one of the lionesses also walked determinedly towards the white cubs, looking very aggressive. Tabby got up from where she had been resting and moved deliberately forward to intercept the lioness, then, having placed herself between the approaching lioness and her own cubs, she started to call them to her.

The Interloper now advanced towards Tabby who raised her head languidly. I was puzzled, for in the past, she used to dominate these lions who, frightened of her, cringed in complete subjection, but today her attitude was almost coquettish. She got up and approached the Interloper and, far from dominating, she lay down in front of him in an almost submissive crouch. There could be no doubt that she was flirting with him.

The time was just before midnight. Much growling and rumbling came from the direction of the bait, yet all the lionesses present were old friends and the noises did not seem to indicate hostility towards each other. Unfortunately, they would not let Tabby's cubs approach the giraffe so they came up to the Land Rover and I fed them scraps.

Meanwhile, the Interloper followed Tabby, nose to tail, seemingly quite unconcerned with anything else that was going on. She flicked her tail and he followed her very closely. I presumed that she must be on heat. Temba noticed and flicked his tail, but in an apprehensive way. I thought he had good reason to worry: if the Interloper really fancied Tabby, the cubs would soon have to fend for themselves, since if their mother mated, she would abandon them. I watched Tabby and the Interloper grimacing at each other; they gave that curious grin called *flemin* which indicates sexual interest. This, however, did not prevent Tabby from coming over to the Land Rover to investigate what I was throwing out to the cubs. The Interloper followed her when she lay down next to the car and he scraped in front of her. Then he lay down about five paces from my left front wheel while Tabby pretended to ignore him and looked away. Meanwhile, the Musketeer was also lying about five paces from Tabby. There was obviously no friction between them. The hostility was between the lionesses of the big sub-pride and Tabby's cubs, not because they were white, I am sure, but because they were so much bigger than their own cubs.

I was thankful to have Jack with me as he kept on whispering in my ear, 'Don't worry, they are not cross. She is not at all angry, she is busy making arrangements for her next family of cubs.' This cheered me up because at the moment there was only a thin wind-screen between me and four hundred pounds of lethal lightning.

Some fighting broke out around the giraffe leg; this is normal over a kill and I couldn't complain because in this case the quarrelling was over a bait. Tabby and the Interloper ignored the noise – they had other things to think about. He was standing over her and she wasn't having any – not that night. It didn't mean she wouldn't mate with him in the future. She was almost certainly just playing the game her way.

Last autumn the relationship had been very different. When he came up wanting some meat, she had snarled and growled at him and he had submitted immediately. I was sure that wasn't going to happen ever again, for the Interloper was now evidently the first in the pecking order. With the two Musketeers he had established himself as a bossman of the pride males. No lion was likely to question his authority for some years to come, perhaps three, even five.

Tabby got up and walked around with the Interloper glued to her behind. She did a lot of tail-flicking to lead him on but no more than that. Both were oblivious to everything around them.

It is extraordinary how strong the mating instinct is. It can be observed in any zoo for instance where birds that are normally very timid and keep well away from people ignore them completely when displaying for courtship purposes.

Tabby now lay down and the Interloper tried to lie near her, whereupon she immediately got up and flicked her tail, at once enticing and repulsing him. A very old story. Finally, the Interloper made a dart and chased Tombi away. I did not think he was angry, simply giving vent to his frustration – what the behaviourists call 'displacement activity'.

Suddenly Dimples appeared and started flirting with one of the Musketeers showing the same sort of friskiness as Tabby had done. I was all the more convinced by this that the three young lions had been accepted by the lionesses as the pride males.

The Interloper roared and was answered by one of the Musketeers and some of the lionesses. One of the former stood over Dimples but she was lying on her side and seemed determined to be uncooperative. Realising the situation was hopeless, the Musketeer walked a few paces and then flopped down.

Tabby's cubs were lying some distance away and making themselves very inconspicuous. It was obvious that they were not going to be allowed near the giraffe. This made it quite clear to me why Tabby had led her cubs to this area and had become a peripheral member of the pride. If she were now to mate, we would obviously have to stand by to feed her cubs. One problem was that the main sub-group had discovered the giraffe and some at least of them had begun to associate the Land Rover with a meal. I was afraid the situation might arise in which we should be obliged to provide two plates daily, one big one for the sub-group and a smaller one for the cubs.

Suddenly Vela came to the Land Rover and looked up at me expectantly. I quickly threw him out some scraps I had left. He got them and carried them over to the other two cubs.

Jack commented, 'Uhlakaniphile impela', which means: He is very clever.

Tabby then came over looking as though she were begging for food but I had none left. I was surprised at how quickly the lions had made the association between the car and food. I only hoped I could condition them as easily to come to the Beethoven tapes.

At around 1.45 a.m. I heard a lioness approaching and, from the way I felt, I was sure it must be Dimples. I dared not look up and instead tucked my head down so that she could not see me. Then, after a few minutes, I decided to head back to camp. I felt we had had quite a night of it and, since I knew that all the lions were well fed, there was no need to worry.

As soon as we moved off, the whites and Vela started to chase the Land Rover – they had certainly attached themselves to us in a big way. I put on a burst of speed to get away from them but Jack said, 'Slow, slow.' We were going to have to drive through the river bed past about eighteen feeding lions, not counting the three cubs chasing us. We drove down into the Maponi, along the river bed for a while and then up the other side. The whites didn't follow us.

It was half past two when we got back to the camp. The date was 2 June and I fell asleep wondering how long it would be before Tabby deserted her cubs. It was certainly looking as if both she and Dimples were rapidly coming on heat again.

And on their own, the cubs would be completely dependent on us for survival.

CHAPTER 13

Beethoven in the Bushveldt

Although we didn't get to bed until three o'clock, Jack and I were up and out by ten the next morning. We had to go into Hoedspruit, the nearest town, to get some fresh fruit and vegetables for the camp and some hessian to put around the Land Rover, partly to protect it from getting more scratched, and partly to conceal its occupants from the lions.

Before I started feeding the lions from the vehicle, they had never paid the slightest attention to it, but now that they had made the connection between it and food we might be in much greater danger. When the hessian was wrapped around the cage, we could cut a few holes in it and through them observe and photograph the lions, but they wouldn't be able to see anybody inside the vehicle.

Hoedspruit is rather like a twenties trading post somewhere in the American mid-west. It has a railway terminal, a huge warehouse in which you can buy anything from a tractor to a needle and thread, a hotel and liquor store combined, and a few small shops. There, too, is the central post office for the area where we have to go from time to time to collect our mail from numbered boxes. In the whole of Timbavati itself there isn't even one single shop, so Hoedspruit is important to us.

On the way there, I dropped in to see Mrs Marula. She said that she had heard me playing the hyena tapes, and had heard the lions feeding on the impala bait and the giraffe all through the night. I promised to give her two rand a day if she succeeded in keeping the children quiet in the early morning, so that we could take some photographs before the lions disappeared into the river bed to hide up and rest during the hot hours. I again asked her not to walk about in the neighbourhood of the feeding stations – this chiefly because Mrs Marula is such a formidable woman and I am convinced the lions are far more frightened of her than we are afraid of them.

Going down the Line road we met Peter and Charlotte at Tryg's. They had been on the phone to Mike Dodds, the cameraman, who was still having visa troubles in Johannesburg. They warned him to bring some lighting equipment with him.

On our return we spent a couple of hours draping the Land Rover in its hessian camouflage. When we had completed the job the vehicle looked very strange.

That night Charlotte and Trish came out with us. As soon as we got to feeding station number one, the lions appeared, looking for meat. I didn't even have to play the hyena tapes; they arrived as soon as they heard the sound of the engine. We fed them immediately, throwing scraps of meat out through the front windows which were not covered in hessian since we needed the visibility. The lions seemed a little nervous, snatching at the meat and carrying it about twenty yards away before settling down to eat. Possibly they were afraid that the other sub-group would once again arrive and chase them off. I kept the Land Rover lights on and used powerful torches as well; I wanted to get them accustomed to bright lights before Mike Dodds arrived with his lighting equipment. Jack thought that it might be the hessian around the Land Rover which was frightening them; it made the Land Rover look different. He may have been right, for till now they had shown no hesitation about eating right beside the vehicle. (After a few days we took the hessian off again.)

Dimples didn't turn up that night; I suspected that she was probably off with her Musketeer once more.

Once or twice during the night we heard other lions roaring, but the cubs didn't show any sign of alarm; and from the direction from which the roaring came, it didn't seem to me that it could have been Phuma's sub-group. More likely it was a strange pride.

At about 12.20, we tried to get some sleep, but it was bitterly cold. We were near a river bed, and in the veldt there is a temperature inversion effect which is startling. The cold air seems to cling to the valleys, so there can be a difference of up to ten degrees between the ridges and the river beds. This is probably why the Africans always build their *kraals* along the ridges, even if it means walking for some distance to get water. The whites on the other hand invariably build their camps right beside the river beds so that they can have easy access to water, but the result is that they are often frozen in the winter and uncomfortably hot and humid in summer.

Having dozed off I woke with a start when some male lions arrived on the scene – almost certainly the Musketeers and the Interloper, but it was difficult to tell in the darkness.

Tabby immediately got up, called her cubs to her and set off in the direction of the Maponi. I watched them until they disappeared down into the river bed. After a few seconds I followed them and caught up with them at the dam, where they were having a drink. Once they'd had their drink, Tabby led them into the thick riverine bush.

It was 2.15 by now and both the girls were asleep in the back of the vehicle. Clearly nothing more was going to happen that night; the lions were well fed and safe for another day so I intended to drive home, but I dropped off to sleep and none of us woke until 6.20 to a beautiful morning, with hot sunshine – very welcome after such a cold night.

As we drove home across the black soil plains, we heard two lots of lions roaring (very unusual at half past seven in the morning) – one pride from my father's farm and the other from a neighbour's land. It could have been Dimples and her Musketeer keeping in touch with the main sub-group, but normally by this time they would have settled down for their day's sleep.

As we went along I shot an impala ram, this time for ourselves, at eighty yards. I got him right between the eyes with the .22 and he dropped like a stone.

From an ecological point of view I had done nothing wrong because he was a young ram, part of a bachelor group, and in no way connected with the breeding stock of an impala herd. Many people object to the shooting of animals as beautiful as impala and giraffe, but the fact is that, in a fenced-in area, they have to be culled otherwise they would eat themselves out of house and home, and with the next drought thousands of them would die.

Happily, if the job is done cleanly, they feel nothing, not even fear. One moment they are alive and the next they are dead. Surely this is far less cruel than death in an abattoir where the beasts have to queue up awaiting their turn for the so-called humane killer, keenly aware of the smell of fresh blood and the feeling of fear that the other cattle exude. A friend who has seen a modern Chicago-style meat factory tells me he can actually smell the fear in the air.

For the same reason it is surely far less cruel to shoot francolin or grouse than to breed battery hens for mass slaughter. Of course, you must shoot straight and never wound an animal. I am prepared to respect a genuine vegetarian but not the hypocrite who enjoys a juicy steak while arguing that it is immoral to shoot game.

We arrived back at Nick Hancock's farm at 9 a.m. Mapique, a new member of the camp staff, had just arrived, our Robert was sitting in Zandy's lap, and Tabs, Jack's Robert and a friend were playing together, a very peaceful domestic scene.

I planned to get some proper sleep in a bed, and then towards the evening go out with some giraffe meat and some impala meat, in the hope that Tabby and the cubs would turn up.

Perhaps by then Mike Dodds might have arrived with his lighting equipment. I wanted to get as many moonlight shots of the lions as possible, but I had no flash equipment; if only I had had some during the previous nights, I could have got some invaluable behavioural shots.

That afternoon he did arrive, with all the lighting equipment we could possibly need. Unfortunately it was now cloudy and also very windy – the worst kind of weather in which to look for lions.

That morning we had butchered the impala I had shot and now large sections of it were simmering in the three-legged black pot over the leadwood fire. We had put a log under the pot and it kept the stew at exactly the right temperature. It would last for at least a week, during which we would add francolin, to give it a dash of extra flavour.

Mike Dodds took to the bush like a duck to water. He thought the impala stew delicious and couldn't wait to go out to look for the lions, so off we went although I knew we should not see any in that weather.

Later, to console himself for having not seen any lions, Mike Dodds took some shots of hyena and other wildlife and we filmed Mrs Marula in her *kraal*. She had a big bowl of fried caterpillars in front of her, and was discarding the heads, preparatory to sharing out the bodies among the children. Caterpillars are regarded as a delicacy in this part of Africa and are full of protein, and thus a valuable addition to any diet.

I translated my conversation with Mrs Marula for Mike's benefit, but when he decided he wanted to repeat a few of the takes, she became impatient.

'Why do you keep asking me the same question over and over again, when I have already answered you?' she asked. That is a problem film crews find themselves up against all over the world.

The next night, 6 June, we found three young males – no doubt the Musketeers and the Interloper – on a kill but had to leave almost immediately because we had two sacks of offal on the tailgate of the Land Rover, and Tabs pointed out that if we approached any closer one of the lions was liable to come snuffling around and with the tailgate open she and Charlotte would be unprotected.

We returned with the tailgate closed and, using artificial light, Mike got some pictures of the lions feeding.

We went back the following morning to see if we could find the lions resting up near the kill. Normally they should have been lying on the open plains near the Machaton but on this day they had broken all the rules and were resting in very thick bush in the one place that is inaccessible to the Land Rover.

The next day we had to drive Peter Dickson to Phalaborwa to catch the plane to Johannesburg after which we took the Land Rover to Neilspruit for servicing. So it was a couple of days before we were able to resume filming.

Tabby, the one member of the pride we could always approach without any fears – a very casual lioness both in her attitude to her cubs and towards humans

The Interloper, who with the Two Musketeers eventually took over from Achilles and Agamemnon, approaches members of the pride. They were by then just beginning to accept him

The Interloper – note his mean eyes

The Musketeers with a lioness from Phuma's sub-group

Tombi appeasing the Interloper

One of the Musketeers appearing to take an interest in Phuma

Suzie Wong, sister of the Two Musketeers, stalking

Feeding time
for the lions:

Tabby about to
tuck in

Phuma, with jackals awaiting
their chance in the background

Vela with his share

Behaviour patterns within the pride:
A lioness submitting to The Interloper

An affectionate exchange of greetings at one of the water-holes

We filmed the sub-group on an impala ram kill then returned later and took shots of the sub-group, including Phuma, resting in the shade, but so far Mike had not seen Temba and Tombi.

While in Nielspruit I had picked up some Beethoven tapes for the next stage in the conditioning process. The following night we loaded the remains of a giraffe on to the trailer – it was about a week old by now and beginning to disintegrate – and we also took the Beethoven tapes.

I now tried out, for our own benefit, the violin concerto which, thanks to John Dunning's amplifier, had a range of about three kilometres: Beethoven booming out over the primeval bush where apart from the engines of the jeeps and Land Rovers, the daily plane we called the Phalaborwa special and the occasional crack of a rifle-shot, the sounds have not changed in millions of years.

By 11.20 p.m. we were on the alkaline plain in the middle of the lions' range – a glorious place which I had known since I was six years old. Soon we had reached feeding station number two where I planned to stop and play hyena tapes. If the cubs came and started to feed, I would then switch over to Beethoven.

The whites soon put in an appearance and smelt the meat on the trailer. The next moment, I felt the Land Rover, the trailer and the two tons of giraffe meat being towed backwards. It is incredible what strength those lion cubs had. Then Vela joined the party. I wished I had had some fresh meat with me because I thought the giraffe must, by now, be too high and probably crawling with maggots. Certainly the cubs, though pulling at it, were not eating it. We had a few pieces of chicken with us which we had meant to eat ourselves, but now I threw them out. I thought the best plan would be for me to find a way of detaching the trailer and leave it where it was which, even if they didn't eat the meat, would pin the cubs down. I might then go off and shoot something else for them. I had no intention of playing the Beethoven tapes till they were actually eating.

The cubs came round the car and one of them started licking the bumper; I could only hope he wouldn't start chewing the tyres. When the moon came up, I thought I caught a glimpse of Tabby but later decided that I must have been mistaken. Probably she was away flirting with the Interloper, and if that were so, she would soon abandon the cubs. Then we would need to feed them; otherwise they would undoubtedly starve since they were not yet old enough to be efficient hunters. Suddenly, Mike noticed that the cubs had started on the giraffe in spite of its condition.

The rest of the sub-group were roaring away but too far to disturb the cubs, so Mike suggested that we should start the Beethoven. I thought the cubs had better become a bit more accustomed to his presence and to the lights and the whirring of his ciné camera. Also I would have been far happier if we had some fresh impala for them instead of the stinking giraffe which they were only eating for want of anything better. Some time around three o'clock, we both suddenly grew very tired and nodded off.

When we woke up at 5 a.m., the lions had gone. We took what remained of the giraffe off the trailer and tied it to a tree, planning to return again that night. In the meantime, I intended to try to track the lions. If I lost the spoor, I would fetch Jack or Mandaban to help me.

The spoor was easy to follow: the lions seemed to have gone into the same area where they had disappeared a few nights earlier. I followed them for a while, through the river bed, but I didn't want to press them too hard at this stage.

Mike and I were certain that Temba, Tombi and Vela had been on their own; obviously Tabby and Dimples were out about their proper business, which is procreation. The cubs were nearly two years old so from now on we could expect her to desert them for ever-increasing periods. If the Land Rover hadn't been around to act as foster mother, they would probably already have left the area and become nomadic.

By ten o'clock Mike Dodds and I were out again on Nick's plains, where we found a zebra kill a few hundred yards from the ecotone of the combretum bush – the ecotone is the fringe area between the thick bush and the open plain. It gives the lions enough cover to enable them to stalk their prey undetected, and yet it is not so thick as to obstruct their movements. The kill was a young zebra. Very little of the carcass was left; the bones had been crunched up, a proof that the hyenas had been there after the lions had gone. There were plenty of vultures around, too, although there was nothing much left for them. It looked as if it was Phuma's sub-group that had made the kill, and I suspected that they would be resting at or near Park Dam, where they would almost certainly have gone for a drink after gorging themselves.

There was spoor of all sorts around the dam – impala, kudu, wildebeest, zebra. Mike asked, 'Why are there not more lion kills around the water holes?' The answer to this is very simple. The lions in this part of the veldt are nocturnal, while the game tend to drink during the hottest part of the day because that is when they feel most thirsty; that is also the time when the lions are asleep.

At night, the game tend to move up to the black soil plains because these are wide open spaces and offer good visibility which is a protection against predators, but also because the plains are about one to two hundred feet higher than the river beds and dams and, therefore, because of the temperature inversion, it is much warmer up there.

In other parts of Africa, even as near as the Kruger Park, a number of the lions hunt in the daytime and there you do find that a high proportion of kills are made around the water holes and dams.

We went off and just by the bullrushes shot an impala, an old ram.

Now we had some fresh meat for the cubs, and as soon as they turned up and were feeding peacefully, I would start playing Beethoven to see how they would react.

CHAPTER 14

A Hard Day's Night

The weeks that followed were a nightmare, literally a nightmare, yet I will remember them with affection and nostalgia for the remainder of my life. I got scarcely any sleep: only perhaps a snatched hour between three and four in the morning, huddled up in a few blankets on the front seat of the Land Rover, or a stolen hour or two in the afternoon and that only if there wasn't an impala to be shot or some poles or cement to be transported to Owl Camp.

In some ways it was the worst time of my life, and in some ways the best. We had one fixed objective: to keep finding and feeding the white lions, whose situation was becoming more dangerous daily while the people who ran the Reserve, and technically owned the lions living on it, decided what they were going to do about them.

We were beset with all sorts of personal problems too. For some weeks we had been commuting between the half finished Owl Camp and Nick Hancock's farm, but now he and his wife were coming down with friends for a protracted stay. Therefore we had to complete our move within a matter of days.

Mike Dodds was still with us looking for herds of buffalo, kudu, duiker, impala, giraffe, elephant, rhino and heaven knows what other varieties of wildlife which he needed as background material for the film. And I had to drive him round; not that this was a hardship, but it took up time.

Charlotte, therefore, very largely supervised the construction of Owl Camp. When, early in June, we made the move, the camp was simple without being primitive. When I made that comment to a friend, he took one look at it and remarked that, on the contrary, it seemed to him that it was primitive without being simple.

As originally planned, there was a circular palisade of reeds and mopani logs about nine feet high and four inches thick about thirty yards in diameter. It had an opening which we covered at night with a wire mesh gate. The tent which I used as office and operational HQ was pitched outside the main camp about fifty yards from the palisade. There I kept all my camera equipment, and my tape recorders and it was fitted with a desk so that I could sort out and label my slides, make notes and transcribe my tapes. Normally, the two Land Rovers were parked somewhere close to my tent.

The long drop was outside the palisade; it had a reed screen on three sides of it only.

In the very centre of the palisade we had placed our three-legged iron pot. There were two, so to speak 'permanent' structures in the camp. Permanent is not a word I like to use lightly because so little in this world is permanent. The main building was an oval-shaped *rondavel*, made of clay and wattle, with a thatched roof and very small windows; the other was no more than a thatched roof on poles, with a cement floor and open on all four sides. It was a very cool spot to sit and eat or drink in the hot weather.

The big building was divided by a screen into two sections. Charlotte had fitted up one with bench seating all around the wall and some local tapestries for decoration; on the floor we had zebra and impala skins. The other section was what might be described as the master bedroom, though it didn't have a bathroom *en suite* as they say in the property ads. It didn't have anything, except a bed, well, not even a bed – a mattress.

Between the main building and the open, thatched shelter was a pantry, also thatched over, where we had a meat safe covered with fine gauze meshing to keep out the flies. Eventually it was to be joined by a kerosene freezer.

On the far side of the camp and separated from these main buildings by a reed screen were two tents – the very latest, light-weight nylon tents with built-in ground sheets and other refinements.

One was intended for Tabs and Robert though as often as not Tabs was to be found curled up at the end of our bed; the other was for our guests. Mike Dodds was the only one when we moved in.

Owl Camp cost between £250 and £375 – and that included all the furniture, crockery, knives and forks, tents. I far preferred it to the £90,000 flat I stayed in when I was in London.

A reliable Land Rover, a good gun, a sturdy camera, a couple of tape recorders – these I must have, for they are the tools of my trade, but possessions scare me because if you are not very careful they soon take possession of you. Half the people in the so-called civilised world are entirely enslaved by their possessions and spend their lives in terror of being burgled. If you don't own anything of value, you need never be afraid of burglars. We packed our few odds and ends and moved to Owl Camp. We left Nick's camp with one lively memory.

Mike, Tryg and I had been out one night feeding the lions and when we returned we found that all hell had broken loose. The Sohebele lions had paid Charlotte a visit, and in the process had wrecked Nick's meat safe stealing three impala that Tryg had shot for me. They'd also gone for Charlotte, which was something she hadn't expected and which made her quite indignant.

The lions were still all around the camp and I asked Tryg to fire off a couple of shots to scare them away. Charlotte then gave us an account of what had happened. She had heard a noise at the meat safe and had presumed that some hyenas were at it, so she went out clapping her hands and shouting in order to shoo them away as she usually did. But, imagine her horror when she found that it was lions who were attacking the safe. They growled and then they went for her. She was astounded and complained to us, 'By rights, lions too should go away if you make a lot of noise. I have never heard of lions that did not run off and these Sohebele lions are not rational, sensible lions. I had to dash inside and lock the door while they knocked the meat safe down and stole all the impala.' She was in fact badly shaken and a drink would have done her good but, unfortunately, our brandy was inside the Land Rover which was by now surrounded by the lions.

Eventually, the Sohebele lions moved away, and we were able to get the brandy and calm Charlotte down. She was far more annoyed than frightened: she gets quite uptight when animals and humans behave unpredictably.

The events of the weeks that followed were largely routine. From the nights I had spent sitting in the Land Rover near feeding station number two, I knew exactly what Tabby's problem was: she was surrounded by lions on all sides. One morning I remember hearing roars coming from five different directions. Tabby had chosen the thick riverine bush along the Maponi as the best place for the cubs to hide up by day. Occasionally she still hunted for them but she was spending a good deal of the time commuting between her cubs and the main sub-group; Dimples was doing the same. This presented us with a number of urgent problems. It indicated that she would very shortly leave the cubs to their own devices, at which point they would become totally dependent on us for food. Also when now she did return to them, she often found them well-fed because they had just dined off a couple of impala supplied by us, while she herself was starving. Moreover, she couldn't hunt because the noise made by the Land Rover frightened away all the prey.

I knew that the presence of the Land Rover was wrecking her hunting but we had to stay with the cubs because Mike Dodds needed some shots of them in the first light of day and, so far, the only way we found of doing this was to follow them all night, wherever they went.

On Friday, 10 June we went to feeding station number two and tried out the Beethoven. It sounded glorious, but it didn't seem to be producing any results. After a bit we took out the Beethoven tapes and tried some hyena ones. The lions arrived almost immediately. It was a dark night but I could see the whites easily as a light-coloured blur against the background.

All three cubs were there. They didn't seem concerned about the lights, but were a little nervy which could have been due to the Beethoven which I had started blasting out at full power as soon as they were eating. However I felt sure they'd soon get used to it.

We heard the Interloper or one of the Musketeers roaring from the Machaton, about three miles away. All the cubs looked up, but remained fairly calm. The next day we tried playing the Beethoven again. The cubs were about thirty yards away and seemed quite unconcerned. It is depressing to realise that this would have to be a regular routine, day after day, or rather night after night, until the Committee had made up its mind about what was to be done.

We had endless discussions among ourselves as to what would be the best solution. On the whole, the general consensus of opinion was that we shouldn't dart one of the whites in case it happened to be injured in the process, but that we should dart Vela, the tawny one. Our thinking was that the three cubs would probably stick together, and that if we could manage to get a radio collar on to Vela we could then monitor him and in that way keep track of all three cubs. But for the moment the radio collar and other monitoring equipment had not yet arrived. It never did.

The following Sunday, we heard the sub-group about half a mile away, so I didn't dare to use the hyena tapes in case it brought them bounding up. Instead, I tried the Beethoven but I don't think they made the connection.

Some hours later, I heard some impala alarm calls which might have indicated the presence of lions, so I switched over for a few minutes to hyena tapes. The roars of the main group had been getting further and further away, down towards the area of the Triangle, too far away for them to be lured.

Within a few seconds Tabby's cubs appeared. The time was about 11.40 p.m. After they had eaten they moved off, and we followed them, using two spotlights in the back, one manipulated by Keith Joubert and one by Mike. They weren't hurrying, just plodding along, their stomachs swinging from side to side, as they always do when they're well fed. Then the Land Rover got stuck in a ditch, and we had to spend quite a time jacking it up from various different directions trying to get it out. This was a bit unnerving with the lions sitting barely fifty yards away, watching us. Keith and Mike kept the spotlights on the lions and warned me whenever it looked as if I ought to nip back in for a couple of minutes.

In all it took about an hour to get the car free. Fortunately, the lions seemed sufficiently interested in my performance not to wander off. As soon as I had got the engine going, they came up and started sniffing around the spot where I had left the torch and the jack. I knew exactly where we were so I could come back to fetch them in the morning.

As soon as the lions moved off, we started following them. They led us a fair old dance that night, crossing and recrossing one particularly difficult river bed four times, and frequently wandering in bush that theoretically was far too thick to take a Land Rover through. Nevertheless we stuck with them all through the night. At 5.10 a.m. they suddenly met up with Tabby again. We heard the low sound she made as she called them. They looked very pleased and a lot of cheek-rubbing and greeting went on. Tabby immediately took over the lead and began to hunt. She was very thin and obviously ravenous.

I remembered a similar incident which happened just before the Musketeers and Suzie Wong left their mother, Golden. They had been on their own for a time, and one day they suddenly linked up with her again, just as the whites and Vela had now linked up with Tabby. Shortly after that, Golden deserted them for good.

The lions settled down to rest at about 7.40 a.m. We had been following them through almost impossible terrain from about 1.30 a.m., a hard day's night.

By 7 p.m. I was back at feeding station number two and the cubs were feeding happily on an impala attached by rope to the back of the Land Rover and exactly five paces from it. Dimples turned up on this occasion and pulled at the impala like a large fish tugging at a bait.

The next day the whites were with the main sub-group in the afternoon. Tryg and I shot a giraffe and loaded it on to the trailer; we planned to tow it to the Machaton so that Mike Dodds could get some shots of the whole pride together. Once again, our victim was an old and ailing giraffe which Tryg had been planning to shoot anyway, so we weren't upsetting the ecology of the reserve.

We towed the carcass to the Machaton and found that Tabby's three cubs, including the two whites, were there, but the remainder

of the sub-group had disappeared, with the exception of the Interloper. Although about the same age as the Musketeers, he was a very
different proposition, larger and heavier than either of them, with a
much broader face. If you were to put it in terms of domestic cats,
you might say that the Interloper had the pug-like features of a
Persian cat, whereas the Musketeers had longer noses, more like
Siamese cats. They took after their father, Agamemnon, and seemed
to us to be far nobler in mien and bearing, better bred, you might
say, than the Interloper. Also, they were basically very quiet, sleepy,
friendly lions, not a bit sinister, whereas the Interloper had very
slanted eyes, with an extremely menacing, evil look.

It was that night I saw the first direct confrontation between the
Interloper and Tabby's cubs: an augury as to what was to happen
more and more frequently in the immediate future.

Vela was crunching the giraffe. The Interloper approached,
crouching very low, and suddenly Vela too crouched low, really
grovelling, whereupon the Interloper stood up regally and growled.
Vela's ears went flat back in abject submission and Temba now
adopted the same cringing attitude.

There was no reaction from the females, Tabby and Tombi, who
went on feeding. This was understandable because as a rule it is only
the young males who are threatened by the pride lions.

Vela was lying quite still, replying to the Interloper's terrifying
growls with little mewing sounds. Suddenly, the Interloper strutted
majestically around in a circle, marking his territory. This was the
first time I had seen him so ostentatiously spraying in front of one of
the lionesses. He rubbed his cheek against a small shrub known as
euclea and then squirted it with urine after which he scraped his hind
legs. We filmed all this which was highly satisfactory, since territorial
markings are fairly rarely witnessed.

Afterwards the lions dropped off the sleep. The Interloper
seemed more interested now in Tabby than in the cubs; probably he
felt he warned them off and could now attend to more pressing
business. He lay down next to Tabby and went into *flemin*, that
grimace that can indicate sexual interest.

At eleven o'clock we left them and went back to the camp to get some sleep, but by half past four that afternoon, we were out again. Tabby and Tombi were feeding on the giraffe and there were vultures in the trees all around. The Interloper arrived but after ten minutes wandered off again. It was clear by now that Tabby had begun to accept the Musketeers, and particularly the Interloper, as the pride males, and it seemed to me that the effects of the social disintegration caused by the disappearance of Agamemnon and Achilles were beginning to wear off. Tabby was becoming more integrated with the pride and starting to use the core area of the range again. We had managed to lure them from the Maponi River to Tongue Plain and from there down to the Machaton. The fact that Tabby seemed sexually attracted to the Interloper and accepted his domination led to her using the core of the range again, which made it a lot easier for Mike Dodds, but raised other problems: principally, the increasing friction between the Interloper and Vela, and to a lesser extent Temba. There didn't appear to be any friction between the two Musketeers and Vela and Temba, but they were members of the same pride, whereas the Interloper was not.

CHAPTER 15

The Interloper Threatens

On Tuesday, 14 June, I decided to let the lions take their chance for one night, and myself have a long sleep, the first in about two weeks.

But, on that particular night, two bull elephants chose to have a pitched battle, right outside our palisade. It wasn't strong enough to keep out an elephant, we knew that, but in the ordinary way we were in no great danger because elephants, like most wild animals, tend to steer clear of recognisable human habitations. However, two enraged bull elephants, probably fighting over a female, were a different proposition. If, for example, one got the better of the other and started to chase him, the pair of them might easily trample down the palisade and demolish everything inside it, ourselves included, without even noticing. If you have ever cut down a large tree and then painfully removed the roots (a formidable task that takes a couple of men a full day), you will have some idea of the enormous strength that elephants possess; they can simply put their foreheads against a tree and push it over, uprooting it as easily as we pull up a lettuce.

We could hear the trumpeting, the thunder of their feet on the ground, and the sickly thuds as they met, head on. There was only one thing to do. We all got out of bed and piled into the Land Rover. An elephant can push over a Land Rover without any bother, but at least we were mobile. I kept the engine running, so that if I saw them approaching I could head off into the bush.

The fight was a spectacular performance and went on for the best part of an hour. Then one of the bulls decided to give the other best, as they put it in prize fight jargon, and slunk away into the bush. The winner, after strutting around trumpeting victoriously for a few minutes, rejoined the herd and we were able to return to the camp and go back to bed.

After a day spent sorting out slides and tapes and carrying out various tiresome chores around the camp, I went out alone on Wednesday, 15 June. I was nervous, as I usually am when I'm out alone, and increasingly so, now that all the lions were relating the Land Rover to the idea of food. I always feel much safer if there are at least two pairs of eyes in the Land Rover and someone with a rifle at the ready.

This time I played only the Beethoven – by now I had switched to the Triple Concerto – and before very long Tombi appeared, walking purposefully towards the vehicle. Then Vela appeared and the Interloper, followed by Temba. It looked as if they had healed their differences for the moment. Now Tabby and one of the Musketeers joined them. The Musketeer ignored the Land Rover, as he had done all his life, but the Interloper watched my every move. He was a dangerous animal and I never felt comfortable when he was around. But he was a beautiful sight: arrogance personified. He walked with a sort of slow-motion, strutting gait, designed to impress other lions. I'm sure it worked; it certainly impressed me.

Then it happened again. The Interloper suddenly started to threaten Vela and Temba. Temba immediately flattened himself, emitting those gentle, placatory, cat-like miaows. Soon, wisely, Vela and Temba decided to remove themselves from the scene for a while, and leave the giraffe carcass to the Interloper.

There appeared to be a certain amount of flirtation going on both between Temba and Tombi on the one hand, and between Vela and Tombi on the other, but I didn't think it was serious; it was probably just a form of play practice, though if this trio should be left on their own, which appeared probable, the possibility of a sexual liaison developing between them would be high. If Temba and Tombi mated, we could hope for more white lion cubs.

Later, when one of the Musketeers started to gnaw at the giraffe carcass, Temba advanced and growled at him, a foolhardy move. But to my amazement, he got the best of the encounter, and the Musketeer stepped down. I can only think that the reason was that they were all from the same pride, and the Musketeer has retained a certain affection for Temba since birth. If Temba had tried that on with the Interloper, he would almost certainly have been killed.

I stayed there most of the night. After a time the lions wandered off into the bush to rest up and the jackals moved in on the carcass, chasing away about a hundred and fifty vultures. I decided it was time to get back to camp for a rest.

When I was next on the plains with an impala it was early in the day. Tabby was the first to emerge, attracted by the noise of the Land Rover and closely followed by the Interloper. Then I came across Phuma and the whole of the main sub-group and, as soon as they got the scent of the impala, they started running after the vehicle. But the Interloper, who had clearly established himself as boss man, chased the others away and had the impala all to himself; it was on a rope, only about four paces from the back of the Land Rover, so I didn't feel too happy about his proximity to me.

What worried me about this situation was that the cubs were obviously on their own again; both Tabby and Dimples were now with the main sub-group. This meant I would have to go out and try to feed them again that night.

While the Interloper was gorging himself on the impala, Scarleg made a mock charge at the vehicle. This was not important in itself but it did show the changing attitude that these animals were taking towards the Land Rover and it made the job a lot more difficult and dangerous.

Later that evening, an hour or two before dark, Jack and I set out for feeding station number two, planning to shoot an impala on the way. We managed to get a ewe, using Tryg's rifle, and it was a heart shot which I don't much like because they always run for a bit after they've been hit, even though they are technically dead. I was getting sick of this daily routine of killing of animals to feed other animals; it was necessary to feed the lions, but I wanted the Reserve to make up its mind finally about what they intended to do with the white lions.

Perhaps here I might describe our travelling film studio, cum armed personnel carrier, cum canteen, cum overnight caravan. Our baggage included the amplifier, which worked off the car battery, which was directly in front of me; a Uher tape recorder supplied by John Dunning beside me (the one I used to play hyena tapes and Beethoven to attract the lions); next to that there was my camera with flash gun and a very powerful hand flashlight. Next in line, a small portable Sanyo tape recorder which I used for making notes. In effect what I did was to record a running commentary of everything as it happened and then extract and transcribe what seemed likely to be useful. I had also a third recorder. This I could either use as a spare or put the Beethoven tape in it while the hyena tape was in the Uher. I also carried some spare batteries.

On the seat I had two guns – my own .22 for shooting impala, and the magnificent .375 Holland and Holland Magnum made by Brno and belonging to Tryg Cooper; on the floor, a loudspeaker which could be mounted on the roof to give maximum volume and range. The roof now had an opening through which I could poke my head for the purposes of photography, and when the opening was not in use it could be closed by strapping over it the seat of an old broken wooden chair, to afford me some protection. My feet were usually surrounded by sliced-up morsels of highly-scented impala meat, and I certainly didn't want any of the lions to try to get at that through the opening in the roof. I also had two thermos flasks of tea at my feet and several ounces of tobacco in my pockets. In the dash pocket, I kept some rolls of film and some spare lenses. We also carried a couple of bags of biltong to chew on if we got hungry, and kept a pillow handy on which to rest the telephoto lens, to minimise camera shake.

In the back, as often as not, there would be Mike with his camera equipment, and Jack. We also carried spare tapes, films, blankets, mattresses, more thermos flasks and biltong and rusks. The tail flap was usually at an angle of ninety degrees with an impala resting on it, and we often had a giraffe attached to the tow bar. Between my legs was a bottle of stout, and in the back, a couple of bottles of wine. All in all we couldn't complain if we were a bit cluttered at times.

On Friday, 17 June, Temba and Tombi came walking through the sunset to feeding station number two and moreover, they came to the strains of Ludwig van Beethoven alone. A few seconds later Tabby showed up, so she was back with them. I had brought a kettle with me to reconstruct for the film the earlier incident with the kettle. I threw it out and sure enough, Tabby started to play with it again, just as she had done when we first found the lions, after losing them for a couple of months. Then the Interloper or one of the Musketeers roared quite close by. They all looked up anxiously, especially Vela, though Tabby continued to play away happily while Temba sniffed at the kettle and carried it off. Tombi chased him playfully for a bit and then stole it from him. Next Temba chased her, but she wouldn't part with it. Temba then started sniffing at her nether quarters and went into *flemin*, so possibly the courtship was more serious than I had realised. If so, this raised the prospect of another generation of white lions.

Next day we had our first big public relations success. I went out with two carloads of visitors and had to put up with endless mockery at the notion that the lions would come to the strains of Beethoven's music. I puffed away knowledgeably on my pipe and kept saying 'You'll see', hoping to hell that the lions wouldn't let me down. I was lucky. As soon as we arrived at feeding station number two with the Beethoven Triple Concerto belting out at full volume, the lions came trotting up obediently and obligingly. We were towing an impala on the end of a rope about five feet long, and Nick and Tim and their guests were impressed by the fact that Vela dragged the Land Rover backwards with all of us in it. At one stage he was so close to the vehicle that Charlotte could have put her hand out through the bars and stroked him. Happily, she resisted that temptation. We noticed that Temba had started growing a white mane, and we were happy to see that Tabby was still with them.

On Sunday, 19 June, Jack and I were out before dawn trying to get the lions to come out on to the plain beside the Mayembule to get some daylight shots of them in the open, but after hours of waiting and tempting them with a mixture of Beethoven and impala, we gave up and returned to camp.

We went out again at sunset and remained out most of the night, but no lions showed up. Later my cousin Alan told me that he had heard the sounds of a kill near my father's camp. So probably Tabby, who had been with them when we last saw the cubs, had succeeded in making a kill for them so that there was no need for us to feed them.

I was up alone all night at feeding station number two, playing both Beethoven and hyena tapes, but again there was no sign of the lions. For two nights they had not come to the tapes, and I began to grow anxious. During the day I met Alan wandering around feeding station number two which probably explained why they had not been there for the past couple of days. It was the worst possible thing he could have done, though he didn't realise it, for the scent of a human would scare the hell out of them. But it was his land, or at least his father's, and I could not forbid him to walk around his own territory.

When, on the following night, I got to where we had staked out the bait I could hear lions roaring on all sides. I tried both the Beethoven and the hyena tapes, but they didn't seem to get any closer. In one way I was relieved because I was alone again and the meat was in the front of the cab with me. There was no way of getting it out to them without opening the door and heaving it out, for it wasn't sliced up into small enough bits to throw out of the window and I hadn't a sharp knife with me.

For two hours I alternated the hyena tape and the Beethoven and, although I kept hearing lions roaring all around me, they never approached the Land Rover. For some reason I was extraordinarily nervous that night; when the flap of one of the tape recorders fell on the seat beside me, I jumped a mile.

By Wednesday, 22 June, I wasn't feeling up to going out and to my surprise Mike Dodds volunteered to go out on his own and try to find the lions and feed them. This was really quite something, because, even for someone as accustomed to the bush as I am, it is very easy to lose one's bearing and this is very dangerous and can be extremely frightening. But Mike found his way to feeding station number two and remained there until half past seven in the morning.

He heard a lot of growling throughout the night and saw several vultures hanging around, which indicated that the lions were probably on a kill. This would explain why they had not responded to the tapes and come to the Land Rover. Of course, during the night, Mike had no way of telling whether it was Tabby's cubs or the main sub-group on the kill, but as he drove back to camp he met Alan, who told him that the white lions had been around his place that night with four others, one of them a large male; that would almost certainly have been Vela, Tabby, Dimples and the Interloper.

It's extraordinary what a difference a good night's sleep can make; the following day I felt ready to tackle anything. So I decided to track down the lions, spooring them on foot if necessary. I was determined to find them again because, although I knew they were safe and well, I wanted to maintain the connection they had made with the Beethoven and with the Land Rover for, before very long we were going to have to dart them and remove them to an enclosure where they would be safe from the Interloper and the other lions. The committee was due to meet in a few days' time and I hoped they would at least reach a firm decision. If they left it much longer, it might well be too late.

I tracked the lions for about three hours and found that the spoor went in among some rocks near feeding station number one. This is an area into which I couldn't possibly take the Land Rover and I certainly wasn't going to go in on foot on my own, partly for fear of scaring them away and partly because it was far too dangerous. It seemed that they had come here because Alan had been wandering all over feeding station number two, so it would be instinctive for them to go to another of the places where they had been fed. Happily, Alan had by now returned to Pretoria, but it might take a few days before they would risk returning. I planned to try to feed them that night at feeding station number one, despite the fact that it was so close to the danger fence.

On the way back I came across an old giraffe, a very old bull in his declining years, almost black in colour, so I shot him as well. I was very sad about this because he was a dear old chap and I knew him well from seeing him around the Reserve, but he was on his last legs and would have died before long anyway, or would have been pulled down by lions.

When we examined the giraffe, we saw that there were claw marks all over his hind-quarters and a bad wound near the tail, which indicated that the lions had already had a go at him. According to my data, giraffe are number two after wildebeest on the list of their food preferences, and during the time I spent observing them, the Machaton pride killed between fifteen and twenty.

Having laid the trail to the giraffe, Jack and I went back to feeding station number one and made a fresh drag trail to feeding station number two. I thought they would probably still be a bit wary of approaching it because of the scent left by Alan, but it was just possible that they might prefer to go there than to where we had left the giraffe, by the bullrushes. At all costs, I wanted to lure them away from the area of feeding station number one.

By now it was about eight o'clock. On our way back to the camp we heard a wildebeest alarm call. There is an interesting point about the different alarm calls made by the various prey animals who browse and graze on the plains. For example, the wildebeest have a sort of snorting alarm call, which doesn't have to be very loud because they move in big herds and can usually maintain visual contact without much difficulty.

The impala alarm call is slightly louder, probably because they use thicker bush and therefore need a stronger call because their visual contact is not good.

The kudu, which live in even thicker bush, are browsers and do not graze and they have the loudest alarm call of all: a beautiful barking sound which on a still day can be heard a mile and a half away. This seems to support my argument that the less visual contact the prey animals have with one another, because of the relative thickness of the sections of the bush they use, the more they need to depend on vocal contact. This might also explain the huge size of kudu ears, which act like amplifiers and are their most prominent feature. Kudu also use a very effective visual signal. As soon as they start to run away, they uncurl their tails, which are white underneath, which is like waving a white flag. The underside of the tails may be seen by all other kudu in the area, and the message is very simple: 'There is danger – run.'

We played tapes for half an hour at feeding station number two, but there was no sign of the lions.

For four nights in a row, we hadn't caught sight of them.

CHAPTER 16

Waiting for a Decision

The next night I was out with Jack again and we spent most of the time keeping the jackals and hyena away from the bait, because we wanted to save it for the lions.

We were getting desperate, so I played the hyena tapes, which was a mistake because it again brought the sub-group trotting up. We watched them for a while and then went on up to feeding station number two to try to lure the whites out. We had more meat in the Land Rover for them. This time we tried both hyena tapes and Beethoven, without any success.

I was worried because this would be my last chance of finding them for some days as I had to go to Nelspruit to have the Land Rover serviced again.

Keith Joubert who is the best living wildlife artist I know had promised to stand in for me, and Tryg had agreed to shoot one impala a day for him and I knew that he was every bit as good at finding them as I was.

In the event, he proved even better. They came for him on the second night and he fed them for the next five nights.

While we were away, the Sohebele lions visited our camp again and stole a lot of things, including my entire stock of biltong. They chewed up the pump we use for pumping the diesoline into the Land Rover; they also tore some of Jack's jerseys into ribbons and generally created a considerable amount of havoc.

We spent our time in Nelspruit buying more stuff for the camp

– a few second-hand chairs, a Calor Gas stove and fridge, which we would need if we were going to have more guests, as now seemed likely.

We also bought a trailer – not in the sense of a trailer caravan, but the sort of thing we could tow behind the Land Rover to cart water from the nearest water hole to our camp.

All in all, it was a very welcome break, after nearly five weeks of work, day and night. But I couldn't wait to get back out into the bush and see how the lions were faring.

On Friday, 1 July, we drove to the Maponi. We were listening to lion roars from quite a distance away and trying to make up our minds which pride they came from when suddenly we heard some frantic baboon alarm calls right beside us. We were parked beside the Maponi, looking across it. I thought they had been disturbed by a leopard or some smaller predator when we heard the first footfalls, and there the lions came – right out of the river bed.

Keith was in the back and so was Mike and they both agreed that we should try to make the lions follow us to feeding station number two and get it firmly fixed in their minds that that was where they should go if they wanted food.

We were lucky. They stuck with us, panting heavily as they padded along. From time to time, I slowed down to let them catch up with us and we could hear them panting all around the Land Rover, although we couldn't always see them. Eventually, when we got them to feeding station number two, we fed them the impala and got some good night shots of them feeding and playing around with the kettle.

Again we spent the whole of the following night out on the plains, but only the sub-group came, and we did our best to keep them from eating the bait. Once again, Tabby had joined the sub-group and was still clearly having an affair with the Interloper. Later we moved to feeding station number one and fed the whites and Vela. While they were eating, one of the Musketeers came up and chased them off which was a very graphic illustration of why they had to stay on the very fringe of the range. One minute the three of them were lying there, happily dining on an impala; the next a

Musketeer arrived and they immediately fled. Because we had seen her earlier with the main sub-group, we knew that Tabby would not be there to defend her cubs, but there was no sign of Dimples either; so they were on their own.

On Sunday, 3 July Tryg shot a giraffe in the morning and that night we were out filming the white lions feeding on it. Once again, they came to Beethoven alone; I was still using the Triple Concerto.

When I got back to camp I encountered a new problem. Because we had a team of Shangaans working on the main *rondavel*, Charlotte and I were sleeping in a tent with Robert, Tabs and the two chickens which Mrs Marula had presented to the children. (One of them incidentally turned out to be a cock and had started trying to crow.) For some reason, these wretched chickens had to sleep in the tent with us. Tabs insisted on it. Charlotte insisted on it. They slept, when they slept at all, which was seldom, in a cardboard box with a lid on it so that they couldn't escape – Tabs' last chicken had escaped and had been eaten by jackals – but they didn't appear to like the box and kept pecking at the walls of their prison. It was a staccato rattling noise like machine-gun fire and it went on all night.

Around this time the Reserve Committee began to discuss building a big enclosure in Timbavati, to provide a safe refuge for the lions. The suddenness of the decision may well have been motivated by considerations other than pure concern for the safety of the white lions, for I heard there had been objections from some of the neighbours about the racket that I was creating by playing Beethoven at dead of night.

The next time we went to feeding station number one we didn't play any tapes because I knew my cousin Bruce was in the camp and would have objected, but the main sub-group came just the same, probably attracted by the noise of the vehicle. Mike did some filming, using sun guns for lighting. This had frightening results, because the lionesses of the main sub-group had not been conditioned to bright lights and didn't like them. Indeed, one of them got so angry when the lights were on her that her tail began to twitch in a most menacing manner, and at that moment she was only two yards from where I was sitting inside a rather flimsy cage. I had my rifle cocked all the time and reversed away before the lionesses had finished eating.

Obviously they now knew about the feeding stations and were determined to exclude the whites from them. This suggested that I was going to have to establish yet another feeding station for the whites in the hope that the main sub-group would not latch on to it too quickly. Unfortunately this would mean going west again, which I wanted to avoid.

I didn't manage to get out again until the night of 7 July. Now I had a new microphone with a parabolic reflector (a sort of collar which fits around the microphone and collects sound over a wide area). With this equipment I hoped to record some sound tracks which we could use for a documentary film.

I set it up beside the remains of the giraffe on a long extension cable and started to play one of the Beethoven tapes. Within seconds the whites appeared. They weren't interested in the giraffe – I didn't think they would be, because it was extremely high – but they took a great fancy to the parabolic reflector and started chewing it to pieces. I pulled in the flex to see if it was still connected (I thought that I might at least have got some interesting sounds on the tape) but I found that they had chewed through that too, so I hadn't got anything.

Tiresome, but it was glorious to see the whites again. Having wrecked the parabolic reflector, they discovered the impala I was towing and were chewing happily on that when the Interloper arrived and squatted on the remains of the reflector, growling menacingly at Temba and Vela. They retreated instantly, where-upon he tore the remains of the impala away from the rope to which it was attached and dashed off into the bush with it.

This showed that all the lions in the area were now regarding us as running a canteen and as a result the task of feeding the whites was rapidly becoming impossible. When the Interloper had gone, the whites reappeared and despondently nibbled at what remained of the carcass but there was little left and it was clear that I would have to leave them, pick up some fresh meat and dash back, hoping that they would still be in the same place.

I did get back later that night, with some fresh meat. I warned the Reserve that the Interloper was threatening Tabby's cubs, in particular Vela and Temba, and told them that there was every possibility that he might soon kill one or other or even both; even Tombi, though female, wasn't safe. The committee's reply was that I should either shoot the Interloper or arrange to have him darted and carried away by helicopter and deposited on another part of the reserve.

This I did not want to do – for a variety of reasons. If I shot the Interloper, who was by far the most powerful and dominant of the three males which had now taken over the Machaton pride, it was unlikely that the two Musketeers would be able to defend the pride against marauding nomads or males from other prides and in the upset that would have followed such a *coup d'état*, the increase in cub mortality would almost certainly be staggering, and result in the loss of all the whites.

If, instead, I had darted and dropped the Interloper in another corner of the Reserve miles away, he might have been attacked by the pride lions ruling the area in which we landed him and would almost certainly have been instantly killed. Alternatively, he might have made his way back to the Machaton (lions are as good as domestic cats, perhaps even better, at finding their way home over enormous distances) in which case my action wouldn't have changed the situation. I therefore rejected both these suggestions.

Instead, I told the Reserve Committee that the white lions were lurking at the very fringe of their range and that unless I could lure them back towards the core, they would soon disappear. This I could guarantee, insofar as it is possible to guarantee anything in the field of wildlife management, and until an enclosure was built the white lions would be walking a tightrope and each day's delay made their fate more problematical.

About this time I heard a rumour that the Reserve was planning to spend nearly $50,000 on fencing for the white lions' enclosure. In my opinion this would ultimately be a waste of money for if the lions were to be preserved and studied and if any serious attempts were to be made to breed from them, they would have to be taken to a zoo where there were geneticists and experts in breeding.

I realised that were I to leave the lions to their own devices for a week, they would probably hang about for that time, to see if there was any more food coming their way. But if it didn't and if there were any pressure from the Interloper, they would disappear probably for ever. Out of loyalty to the whites, I went on spending my nights feeding them. For three nights they came to the sound of Beethoven alone but this did not prove that they were becoming conditioned to the music; they might have just seen the lights of the Land Rover or heard the engine. Indeed, on a couple of nights, they had come to the sound of the Land Rover alone. Usually I lured them initially with the hyena tapes; they didn't have to be conditioned to those sounds. Evolution had done that over the centuries.

On 12 July, only Tombi turned up. She immediately grabbed a piece of meat and ran into the bush with it. We never saw her again that night; plainly she was terrified of something. Where were the other two? They might already have left the Reserve, though I believed there was such a strong bond between Tabby's three cubs that they would stick together, whatever happened.

On the other hand, the two males could have been killed by the Interloper. Meanwhile, the Reserve Committee's plans were being made on the assumption that the status quo would remain till they were ready to reach their decision. They were reckoning without Africa, where the rules that govern the bush are much more ancient and uncontrollable in human terms than any plans made by twentieth-century man.

I was alone in the camp with Mapique on 13 July, when we heard a lion roaring very close; it sounded to me like one of the Musketeers or the Interloper. A few seconds later Mapique came to me and said, 'Hey, there's something moving out there.' He was loading the Land Rover and had seen something in the beam of his flashlight. I went out, and there were the white lions, crouching around the Land Rover waiting to be fed. We jumped into the vehicle, which fortunately had been loaded with some fresh meat, drove about thirty yards from the camp and fed them there. An interesting fact was that I had been playing some Beethoven, for my own entertainment. So, possibly, they came to the music. On the other hand, it may have been only a contributory factor, because we had been dragging various animal carcasses backwards and forwards between the camp and the plains and there must have been scent trails leading to the camp from all over the area, so they may have found Owl Camp by following up one of the scent trails.

It was now clear to me that the Interloper was mating with Tabby and that we could expect a litter of cubs. The chance of these being whites was not high, for the recessive gene existed in only one of the parents, since the Interloper was from an outside pride.

I had also seen Temba trying to mate with Tombi. If that proved fruitful there would be a much higher chance of there being some white cubs in the litter. If Temba had reached the age at which he was beginning to get randy, it is quite possible he might have tried it on with Tabby, which would probably account for the Interloper's antagonism.

Even though we had been out, night after night, we had now lost touch with the lions for several days. We tried both the hyena tapes and the Beethoven and finally, in desperation, I even tried Mozart, on the advice of a friend who said that, as the lions were growing up, Mozart might appeal to them more, since human music lovers tend to graduate from Beethoven to Mozart and thence to Bach. Alas, the lions didn't appear, even for the Elvira Madigan theme.

Once again, Jack made an inspired suggestion: 'If you want to find the white lions,' he said. 'Why don't you try around Mrs Marula's? I've a feeling that's where they are.'

So, on 16 July, I went to Mrs Marula who said, 'I saw the lions last evening, the white ones, just as the sun was going down. At first they didn't do anything. They just came into my *kraal* and sat down over there and the dog was barking at them. Then they dragged away my bath and my cooking pots. They dragged them all over the place – I think they were only playing, but the dog got frightened and ran to Moskin's *kraal* and I went inside and shut the door. They stayed here for quite a while, and then walked off down the road. There were three of them, the two whites and the brown brother. I didn't see the lioness, the mother, but I could hear her close by, calling to them, Mm, Mm, like that.'

So Tabby was visiting her cubs, at least from time to time; that was a consolation.

The Reserve Committee still hadn't made up its mind what to do about them.

CHAPTER 17

D-Day: The Plan of Campaign

On 18 July we established feeding station number three, more or less due south of feeding station number two, on the southern edge of Tongue Plain, and as far from Joubert's fence as feeding station number two, but on the very southern fringe of the Machaton range, in an area where I hoped the Interloper would not discover them, at least for some time.

We had only been there for twenty minutes when they came out of the bush in response to the Beethoven tapes.

On the following night, we went there again but the Interloper arrived so of course the whites failed to show.

This opened up the argument again as to whether I should shoot him or dart him. By now I had thought a lot more about the subject, and my arguments against either course were even more cogent.

At this particular time, the Machaton pride was dominated by three male lions, one fully grown and very formidable – the Interloper, and two very nearly fully grown – the two Musketeers. All around the Machaton range were other prides with their own pride males, in most cases two; in particular, there was a pride to the north with two magnificent pride males. If the Interloper were removed, the Machaton pride would immediately become vulnerable because the two pride males to the north would only have the relatively juvenile Musketeers to deal with, instead of a powerful triumvirate.

But why should the males to the north want to take over the Machaton when they had a pride of their own? Because the Machaton range in terms of prey was – and still is – the choicest in the whole Reserve. It is one of the only ranges in the Reserve where there is a year-round supply of game. This would explain why the previous two pride males, Agamemnon and Achilles, were such outstanding specimens. I have been looking at lions all my life and you would go a long way, not only in the Reserve, but in the whole of Africa, to find two lions as magnificent as that pair were in their prime. The competition for that range is so fierce that the strongest, the biggest and the most handsome lions will always end up in charge of it.

If the Interloper disappeared and the Musketeers were routed, cub mortality would increase immediately, with the strong possibility that Phuma would be lost. The Musketeers, too, would have been obliged to become nomadic, so that the white gene they carried would have been lost to the Machaton pride. Finally, as far as Temba and Tombi were concerned, they would have found themselves in precisely the same position, because the new pride males would immediately harass them, just as the Interloper was doing, not because they were white, but because of their age. In fact, removing the Interloper would have meant interfering with nature in a big way and could only have ended in disaster.

But, because he had now discovered feeding station number three, I had to set up yet a fourth feeding station, further to the west, and near the boundary of the Reserve. The situation was well illustrated one night when there were lions roaring to the north, to the east, and to the south, so that it was obvious that the white lions would probably go west, in both senses of the word, unless the Committee made up its mind pretty quickly.

Mike Dodds returned on 19 July and we drove along the Line road to Tryg's to make a telephone call. It turned out to be an extremely useful exercise, as it happened, because four hundred yards from the danger fence we saw the spoor of the white lions veering off toward Fanie Nel's land, so at least we knew roughly where to go and look for them that night.

We returned to the area about eleven o'clock with an impala fastened to the back of the vehicle by a chain. I foolishly opened the night's programme by playing a few hyena tapes because I didn't think the Interloper could possibly be anywhere within earshot. The tape was answered almost immediately by a roar from him. It was beginning to look as if he had been spooring the white lions, or Temba and Vela, which was why he came to be so far away from the rest of the main sub-group and in the exact place where Tabby's cubs were hiding. Plainly he meant business. That settled it. From now on, I was determined to stick to Beethoven. If the whites didn't arrive, there was nothing I could do about it; but I now knew that if I played hyena tapes the Interloper would soon show up, and if he was anywhere around, there was no chance that the cubs would emerge from their hiding place.

At long last, the Reserve Committee came to a decision and on Friday, 22 July a team was engaged to start building an enclosure to house the lions. It was to be built on a neighbour's land, near Tryg's house, because the Game Warden was the ideal man to look after the lions in captivity.

Until it was built, it was up to Jack and me to go out every night, find the lions, feed them and try to keep them inside the Reserve.

I had to combine feeding the lions with Mike's filming. One incident we hadn't yet achieved very effectively was a reconstruction of the kettle affair. So, one night, when we had Mapique with us as well as Jack, I threw the kettle out for the lions to play about with, but for some reason they weren't interested. Then the light wasn't right and Mike's magazine had run out, so Mike demanded another take. I got Jack to nip out and fetch the kettle back, while the lions weren't looking. I then drove back to where they were and threw it out again. Jack retrieved it happily enough three times – he is extremely brave when working close to lions – then suddenly he reached his limit, and when I asked Mapique to hand it to me yet again, he exploded. 'No, don't you give that thing to him any more,' he said. 'He'll only throw it out again and I've already rescued it three times with all these bloody lions around. I see no point in all this nonsense.' Like Mrs Marula, Jack was not convinced of the necessity for all this repetition.

During these days it became clear to us that it was no longer just the Interloper who was trying to exclude Tabby's cubs from the pride. On more than one occasion we saw one of the pride lionesses going for them; basically, and understandably enough, they were protecting whatever supply of food was available for their own much smaller cubs. We also established beyond doubt that the lions would come to Beethoven alone. There was even a night when I think they came purely to visit me, or possibly because they were hooked on Ludwig Van. They certainly weren't hungry; they had had an impala and a half the night before and were as fat and bloated as overfed domestic cats.

The operation was now drawing to a close and I was beginning to feel a vacuum opening up in my life.

The men were now hard at work on the enclosure near Tryg's house. It was supposed to be completed around 29 July, and soon afterwards they would want me to dart and capture the lions. They hadn't told me what the lions' ultimate fate was to be, though now that the news of their existence had got around, the government was very insistent that they should not be allowed to leave South African soil.

On 23 July I went to have a look at the workmen constructing the lion-proof compound which I had christened Sing-Sing. It was to be about nine feet high, with overhangs so that they could not climb out. The support poles and the wire netting were sunk about a foot and a half under the ground in concrete to prevent them from digging their way out, and there was to be a second fence around it about five feet high. There was a water trough inside, and plenty of shade, and Tryg had cleared areas under the trees for them to lie around in comfort. The enclosure was about half a hectare in area.

On my return journey, I saw lion spoor right beside the danger fence, and at one point it was clear that they had gone in under it. We saw some white fur on the barbed wire, proof as positive as it is possible to get in this part of Africa. It was almost possible to be

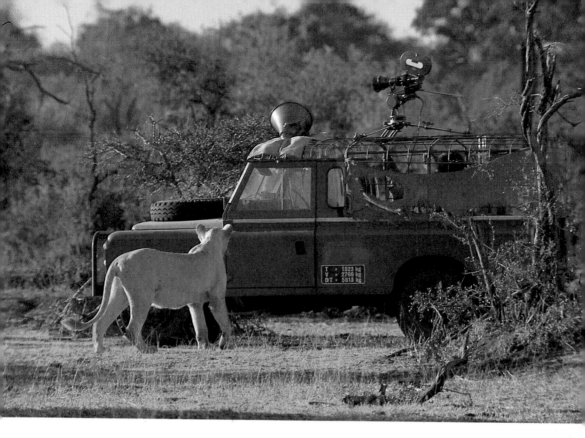

The white lions beginning to get hooked on Beethoven

Night after night, at this stage, I had to go out and feed them:
Vela in a playful mood appears to prefer our kettle to meat

Tombi eating, with Vela,
awaiting his turn

Temba, always the first to arrive

Tabby and her three cubs enjoying a meal

Temba and Tombi sharing a joint

Temba, immobilized immediately after being darted

Petri Viljoen removing the dart

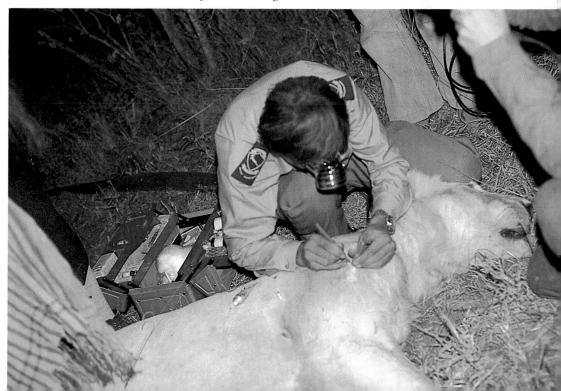

Jack looking at Temba by now so completely knocked out by the drug that Tabs could examine his teeth at close range

All three cubs immobilized

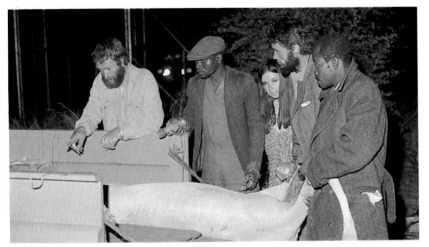

loading them on to Keith Joubert's pick-up

on their way to the enclosure

The lions' enclosure
which I christened
Sing-Sing

Vela and Temba inside
it – and safe at last

as positive about the spoor: that of two almost fully grown lions and the slightly smaller spoor made by Tombi.

Now I knew for certain that the whites were being pushed out beyond the fringe of the Reserve into the land of the farmers and their guns. If it was not already too late, with the Beethoven and some fresh impala, I could perhaps lure them back into the Reserve and hold them for a few nights more, but that was about the extent of it.

Everything now depended on how quickly the enclosure was completed.

We were coming up to the last act of Operation White Lion.

Our feeding station plan, designed to lure them away from the danger fence, had been wrecked by the fact that the Interloper and the rest of the sub-group had cottoned on to it so quickly that we had had to retire, with the white lions, to the extreme western fringe of the range, right up against the fence. But at least I had succeeded in conditioning the cubs to come to Beethoven alone, which meant that when the day came to dart them, we could be pretty certain that the music would attract only the whites and Vela, and no other lions. We had evidence, from the spoor, that they had, attracted by the Triple Concerto, travelled as far as one mile to the Land Rover.

By Monday, 25 July, well ahead of schedule, the enclosure was complete – a hideous structure, like a concentration camp, all gleaming silver poles and silver wire meshing, with an overhang inside of barbed wire at a 45 degree angle, a most sinister-looking arrangement. It was going to be very sad to see the cubs in there and I hoped it wouldn't be too long before they were moved to an open-air zoo, where they would be properly looked after.

We now had a meeting to plan the darting procedure in detail. We called it D-day for Darting-day. It was held at Tryg's house and those present included Tryg and Petri Viljoen. I wanted Petri to do the actual darting as he had had plenty of practical experience of this pretty tricky operation. In the previous few months he had successfully darted more than thirty lions in the nearby Sabie Sands Private Nature Reserve. We had decided to dart all three cubs. I was not going to leave Vela on his own in the bush; he wouldn't have lasted a week.

The plan of campaign was that on D-day afternoon at two o'clock everyone concerned in the operation would assemble at Owl Camp for a full-scale dress rehearsal. We broke the operation down into three phases.

In my original jeep, which we had repaired for the film, would be Charlotte, myself, Tabs and Jack. We would have an amplifier working off a spare twelve-volt battery, and I would play the Beethoven Triple Concerto through a loud-hailer placed on the roof, to lure the lions out of the bush. I would also have some slices of meat to throw out to them to keep them pinned to the spot.

I would first drive the jeep to a predetermined spot – the place where we considered the lions most likely to be. We would have selected this spot by spooring them – assuming we could find the spoor. Alternatively we'd go by Jack's instinct.

In my diesel Land Rover, which would be driven by Tryg following the jeep, Petri Viljoen would travel with his two dart guns, one operated by gas for close range work and one operated by cartridge for firing over longer distances. He would have at least ten darts loaded with Sernalyn, and they would have varying dosages, slightly smaller ones for Tombi. Petri was confident that he could estimate the weight of all three lions pretty accurately from their ages; after all, he had been darting and weighing lions of known age for several months. The Land Rover would be parked in the pre-arranged position and Tryg would work a spotlight and also stand guard with his ·375 Magnum rifle.

When lions are darted, they sometimes run a short distance before collapsing, so one of Tryg's jobs would be to follow each darted lion with his spotlight and mark the exact place where it dropped. He would also be watching out for strange lions and if any turned up and showed any signs of attacking Petri or mauling one of the drugged cubs, he would have to be prepared to shoot. But this would only be a last resort: he would first try to dart any strange lions that appeared.

In my little jeep, Jack would have another spotlight, and it would also be his job to keep the light on each lion as it was darted and mark the spot where it fell, so we would be doubly covered on that score.

Mike Dodds, with his camera mounted on a tripod on the roof, would travel with Tryg and Petri and would film the whole scene from there. Keith Joubert would be there too; he would operate the sun guns and other lighting equipment. Finally Mapique would also be on board ready to help in case of need.

The little jeep would go to Point X and park. The Land Rover would follow it and park parallel to it, on the right of the jeep and about seven paces away. We had already done a good deal of filming in similar circumstances, using both the Land Rover and the jeep, and on two occasions when we had them parked parallel like that the lions walked in between the vehicles without any hesitation.

The plan was that as soon as we were in position, I would start up the Beethoven tapes. Hopefully the lions would soon arrive and we would throw bits of impala down between the vehicles.

This would give Mike the best possible conditions for filming and should also make it far easier for Petri to dart them accurately. We planned to dart Tombi first, because she's the most wary, then Temba and finally Vela.

We had decided to do the darting at night for a variety of reasons. For one thing, the lions were accustomed to coming out of the bush at night in response to the Beethoven tapes – they rarely came out during the day.

We could have adopted our old practice of sticking with them until dawn to get the advantage of daylight both for the darting and for the filming, but it is hard enough to follow lions around all night in one Land Rover, and with more than one vehicle it would have been out of the question.

Petri had also explained that he would much prefer to do the darting at night because of the lower temperature. When lions are drugged, they can no longer pant to expel heat, so if you dart them in the daytime, you have to leave them in a shady spot and keep dowsing them with water, which complicates the operation.

We also discussed whether we ought to bring a vet along, but Petri was confident that he could handle the situation; he had, he said, all the drugs that might be needed if anything went wrong: anti-biotics to prevent the wounds from becoming infected, and an ointment for their eyes and ears. The eyes, for example, might remain open, in which case a special protective ointment would he used. It was obvious that Petri had researched the operation so fully that we had no need to worry about his side of it.

As soon as all three lions had been darted and Petri was satisfied that the drug had taken effect, Jack, Mapique, Keith and I would drag them and lay them out together in a position about eight yards behind the Land Rover.

Phase II would involve a couple of back-up vehicles. We had borrowed a walkie-talkie radio, so theoretically at least, we would be in constant radio contact with the whole party. Keith Joubert's open Toyota pick-up truck, driven by his wife, Frances, would be parked about a quarter of a mile away from Point X. Also parked about a quarter a mile away would be a neighbour's closed-in Volkswagen, filled with his guests.

When the lions were laid out behind the Land Rover, I would call Frances on the walkie-talkie, and she would then drive to Point X and back up the Toyota to the place where we had laid out the lions. Mike would have his camera mounted about six yards away to film the loading and we arranged who were to be the loaders and the precise positions they would take, so that there would be no muddle at the last minute. Petri said the loaders would have to wear plastic gloves, because lions frequently carry a little bug, a variety of *echino coccus*, which can be extremely dangerous to humans.

We decided to load the two whites in Keith's Toyota; and since there was plenty of room in our neighbour's Volkswagen we decided to let him transport Vela to the enclosure.

Because Charlotte and Tabs had been so intimately connected with Tabby's cubs ever since they were born, they naturally wanted to help with the loading. Eventually it was arranged that the loaders would be Charlotte at the head, Tabs at the tail, Jack and myself in the middle, with Mapique standing in the Toyota to receive the lions. For the dress rehearsal, we would use an impala as a stand-in for the lions.

Keith and Frances would be in the cab of the Toyota; in the back would be Charlotte, Tabs, myself and Jack, as well as Mike with his camera and Mapique holding the sun gun – quite a load along with two almost fully-grown white lions.

Phase II would end as we left for the new enclosure beside Tryg's house.

Phase III would be the arrival at Sing-Sing, and the unloading of the lions inside the enclosure, and would entail a thorough examination of the lions by Petri. This particular phase would not end until the lions had fully recovered from the drug – it normally wears off in about eight hours.

That was the plan. I wasn't naive enough to believe that it would go exactly as we had envisaged because there were so many imponderables involved even leaving aside the fact that this was Africa, where everything always goes wrong.

But at least we now had a plan.

CHAPTER 18

The End of the Affair

The dress rehearsal that night went without a hitch, so we decided to stay out and, if the lions did appear, we would go ahead and dart them because they might not turn up again for a couple of nights and every hour was becoming crucial if we were going to be able to rescue them.

On the evening of 25 July, I led the procession of four vehicles through the Machaton, where we heard the main sub-group roaring. We now knew where they were and so could avoid attracting their attention by not pointing the loudspeaker in their direction, though I was confining myself to the Beethoven tapes and I didn't think that any of the sub-group, with the possible exception of the Interloper, had so far made any connection between Beethoven and free meat.

We went first to my father's dam, where we practised the loading drill with the impala and tried out the walkie-talkie apparatus which worked perfectly.

I had a feeling that the lions were probably somewhere in the region of Johnnie's Dale, but decided to try my father's dam first on the off chance that they might be around there. It is a more open area and therefore better both for darting and for filming.

I had an impala – the one we had used as a stand-in for the lions – tied to the front of the jeep, between the spare wheel and the windscreen, and as I went through the Mayembule river bed, the moon came out, lighting up that whole fantastic landscape . . . the twisted knobthorn trees, the umbrella-like shingayis, the combretum bush, the black Dolorite plains. It was a beautiful night, cool without being chilly, an ideal night for luring out the lions though I couldn't help thinking, with a heavy heart, that this might well be the last time.

We went through the river bed, not very far from my father's camp, Vlak, where we had been living when we first saw these lions. I found the smell of the freshly killed impala very pleasant indeed. Most people would find this rather bizarre, but perhaps it's got something to do with my childhood memories.

I knew every inch of this land: I had been walking over it for thirty years, in fact since I was about six. On the Line road, which is as straight as an airport runway, I could see the three sets of headlamps of the other vehicles following me.

I passed my father's camp and the old leadwood tree I remember so well from my childhood; it must be at least five hundred years old which means that it was already growing here when Columbus discovered America.

We tried the vicinity of my father's dam for about two hours before moving south-west in the direction of Johnnie's Dale. I had to put up with the usual sarcasm about the idiocy of expecting the lions to come to Beethoven. Only Keith, Jack and Mike Dodds knew that it worked, but Jack was a bit doubtful for he had a sneaking suspicion that they would have come to the Land Rover anyway because he believed that lions always knew instinctively ('in their hearts', as he put it) where meat was to be found.

When we reached Johnnie's Dale, I tried the Beethoven tapes again with no success. The only creature which emerged from the bush there was an old hyena which often hung about the Land Rover; I suspect that he, too, was now firmly hooked on Beethoven.

We went on playing the tapes from various positions until after 3 a.m., then gave it up and went our various ways, having arranged to try again that afternoon. We weren't too disappointed. This expedition had only been intended as a dress rehearsal.

When we left Owl Camp the next day at about four o'clock, Charlotte suggested that we should go back to Johnnie's Dale, to a place where we first saw lions when we went to live at Vlak. I had, of course, been seeing lions down here all my life, but these were the first lions that Charlotte had seen at Timbavati. We hadn't seen enough of them at this stage to know whether they were the Machaton lions; probably not, because Johnnie's Dale lies outside the fringe of even their extended, rainy season range. Jack now had a strong feeling that we would find them there and an equally strong feeling that if we didn't find the lions and dart them that night, it would be too late.

'If you don't find them tonight, Chris,' he said to me, 'I don't think we're ever going to see them again.'

The Drakensburgs looked spectacular silhouetted against the setting sun as we drove to the far south-western corner of the range and beyond it. I had my full complement of personnel in the little jeep, and so had Tryg in the Land Rover that followed behind me. The others had not turned up by the time we left the camp, so I had left them a note telling them to wait at my father's camp until they heard from us, and suggesting that if they should come across the white lions they should feed them at once and try to get in touch with us on the walkie-talkie. If, in the meantime, I managed to lure out the lions, I planned to pin them to the spot with an impala and stay with them, while Tryg and Mike went back to Vlak to fetch the others if the walkie-talkie let us down, as I suspected it would.

We passed a huge giraffe standing beside the Line road, looking a bit puzzled at the sounds of Beethoven which were issuing from our loudspeaker, then drove through the Machaton and headed west across the alkaline plains. There were no signs of any lions on the plains and we didn't hear the main sub-group roaring, though it was still a bit early. Once again I had the impala on the front of the car between the spare wheel and the wire mesh windscreen. It was a day older now, and smelled it.

We passed the ant heap where the lions had played games with our kettle on that night, so long ago it now seemed, when we found them again after they had been missing for that agonising couple of months. We saw a big herd of impala right up in the apex of The Triangle, and then drove past the bleached bones of a giraffe kill – the one featured in *The White Lions of Timbavati*, with Phuma acting king of the castle.

152

All along the way I kept passing places of significance in terms of the life of these lions. Normally it wouldn't have occurred to me to give them a thought, but that night I was feeling sentimental – I think we all were. At one point between the Mayembule and the Maponi you can see almost the whole of the lions' range, and we all had memories associated with almost every antheap and tree in the area. We could also see the little rocky *kopje* or hillock beside the Kruger National Park fence. There's a cave there which was inhabited, towards the turn of the century, by a hermit called Mayembule, who gave his name to the river. He lived by hunting, using only a bow and arrows or a spear.

We had by now reached the area where Charlotte saw her first Timbavati lions back in February 1975. We tried for a while, without success, at a spot just over the boundary of Johnnie's Dale, on a farm owned by Walter Piel. When they failed to show up, Charlotte suggested we should try a bit further north, near a little river that runs along between Fanie Nel's and André Marais' land. Here again, we tried the Beethoven tapes without any success. Charlotte's instinct seemed to have deserted her.

I then sent the Land Rover back to Vlak because Tryg had a bad cough. Whenever I had been out with the lions and someone in the vehicle has coughed suddenly, they have immediately run away, and I didn't want that to happen now. I took a second impala from the Land Rover and fixed it in front of the impala I already had on the bonnet. I planned, if I found the lions, to throw off one impala to keep them occupied and then, if the walkie-talkie didn't work I could drive back to Vlak and collect the whole team while the lions were busy with the first impala. I would then feed them the second, and we would proceed to carry out the darting phase of the operation.

I sometimes find it difficult to explain to people why you must always whisper and never cough when observing these lions from a jeep or Land Rover at very close range. If they don't mind the Beethoven, or the noise of the Land Rover's engine, or the crashing of broken branches as I burst through the bush after them, why should they be afraid of a snatch of conversation or a cough? The answer is very simple. Most animals, lower than the primates, are controlled very largely by genetic programming and the only way that genetic programming can work is by instilling in them an instinctive fear of the known. Fear of the unknown only comes later, with the cause-and-effect reasoning mind, which baboons, for example, seem to possess to quite a marked degree.

Lions know and fear humans and if they hear a voice or a cough, they instantly recognise the sound as human, as something to be feared, and consequently they normally run away, but they have not had the time to acquire any knowledge of motor vehicles or of Beethoven and therefore have no fear of them.

By now it was about ten o'clock and I planned to stick it out at this point until midnight, in order to give the lions a chance to hear the music and, if they heard it, and were hungry, make their way to the vehicle. The range of the amplifier, as far as the lions were concerned, was about three kilometres, so I had to give them ample time to hear it, make the mental connection and then find the Land Rover.

If they didn't come by midnight, I intended to try one more area from midnight until about three o'clock.

At 11.25, we moved back to the spot in Johnnie's Dale where Jack had suggested I would find them. He has such an uncanny instinct about these things that I felt sure they must be in the area. Then I heard the Interloper roaring somewhere nearby and realised that probably they were there but were refusing to come out of cover because the Interloper was snooping around. However, we decided to stay there for an hour or two.

By now, we were down to the original team: Charlotte, Tabs, Jack and myself. A good combination of complementary skills – the instinctive reactions of Charlotte and Jack, plus the knowledge I have picked up about lions by reading about them and by studying their behaviour in the field; Jack's utter confidence when working out in the open in the immediate vicinity of the lions; and my ability to drive the Land Rover out of a tight corner in a hell of a hurry if the need should ever arise; Jack's speed and skill in slicing up impala; my accurate shooting to bring them down cleanly; Charlotte's ability to

154

tell the lions apart, even at dusk and over a great distance. All in all, quite a formidable team. Tabs by now had fallen asleep and Charlotte was feeling drowsy. Jack and I were sharing a thermos flask of tea.

'Did you hear that?' I asked Jack, suddenly. 'Impala alarm calls. This just might be it.'

I turned up the Beethoven but even over the noise of the Triple Concerto we could hear the thunder of fleeing hooves.

'They are approaching this place,' Jack said, quietly and confidently.

We heard impala alarm calls, we heard zebra alarm calls, and the next minute a herd of zebra came rushing past the Land Rover, just missing it.

For a few seconds nothing happened. I thought it was yet another false alarm. Then I turned down the Beethoven and we listened carefully. We could hear something rustling in the undergrowth. Then I saw the familiar pale, shadowy forms emerging from the bush.

It was the whites!

Of course, the walkie-talkie wasn't functioning, as I knew it wouldn't when we needed it most, so there was nothing for it but to poke my rifle through the windscreen and push the impala that was resting on the spare wheel to the ground. Vela grabbed it immediately – he remained, to the last, by far the smartest of the three – and the other two advanced on the second impala which was wired to the front of the vehicle, so I had to back out of the place at considerable speed. They chased me for a bit, but I soon shook them off. I was counting on the fact that they would return to Vela and either be granted, or seize, a share of the meat and stay there until I could get back with the support team.

I reached Vlak in record time and told the others to follow me. I thought they were right behind me, but on leaving Vlak they must have turned right instead of left, because we couldn't see any sign of headlamps behind us. This meant that I would have to take a link road and go like the hammers because I wanted to cut them off before they blundered into the lions and frightened them away again.

I managed to cut them off at the point where the link road intersects the road that they had taken but this now meant approaching the lions from the wrong direction. On the western side of the point where I had left them, the terrain was very open, which would have made it ideal both for darting and for photography. However, as it was a very small impala I had given them, there was a danger that the lions would have completely demolished it and disappeared if we took the longer route around to approach them from the west. We would just have to make the best of it.

We followed the plan that we had so carefully rehearsed the previous night. I approached the spot first, in the little jeep, playing the Beethoven to reassure the lions. I had to stop a fair distance away from where I had left them, because we had to get out and unwire the impala. However, I reckoned that by playing the Beethoven at full volume and shining the spotlight on the impala, we could probably entice them to come to us.

It worked perfectly. Once again Vela was the first to arrive, followed by Temba. They entered the space between the little jeep and the Land Rover without any hesitation and started to tear at the impala carcass.

Now over to the tape, which conveys the tension of the occasion better than a description written afterwards in cold blood.

CHRIS: There's Temba, only two feet away from me. Petri standing up in the Land Rover, getting his dart gun ready. The lions have dragged part of the impala to about two paces in front of the jeep. Petri is aiming now, he's aiming to dart. That's it, the dart's gone into Temba, spot on, in the right shoulder. Temba is turning round and trying to chew at the dart with a surprised look on his face rather like a fighting bull when the first *bandillera* goes in. Oh, Christ, I feel terrible. Temba doesn't seem to be too worried, he didn't try to run away at all. But where's Tombi? She hasn't shown up yet.

Now Temba's sitting down looking at me and I can see the dart hanging from his right shoulder. I feel terrible. I'm shaking all over. Where's Tombi? No sign of her yet.

CHARLOTTE: In my whole life I've never felt so emotionally

drained. These beautiful animals being darted, going to be put in a cage. I know it's the best thing for them, the only thing, but it does seem so terrible.

CHRIS: Temba is beginning to pant now. Still no sign of Tombi. Don't stand up too much, they're very nervous. Ah, there's Tombi now, remaining in the background, about twenty yards away. I think she senses that something strange is happening. Petri's taking a chance and aiming at her at that distance and there it goes – a dart right into Tombi's shoulder and she's running away. Temba is lying down gently. Tombi has collapsed. She started to run away and then just collapsed.

Jack is shining the spotlight on the two whites in turn. Temba looks all right, and so does Tombi, but of course it's too early yet to say. Tryg is firing an airgun at a hyena – it's the one that's hooked on Beethoven – to frighten him away because he was getting a bit close. No sign of Vela for the moment, but the whites are safely darted and are both down.

Jack has just remarked in Zulu that they look as if they have been drinking *jubula*, the local beer. The time is 1.15 a.m. and both Charlotte and Tabs are in tears.

Here comes Vela, lying down right in front of the Land Rover where he has so happily rested so many times. It makes it a dead easy shot for Petri who is now aiming. That's it, there it goes. Smack in the right shoulder again, for the third time. The lions are all moaning gently. I can hear the Interloper roaring but he seems to be a long distance away. Vela is shaking his head from side to side, trying to shake the dart out. The whites have staggered to their feet and collapsed again. This drug takes about an hour to achieve its full effect. We're still playing the Triple Concerto in the hope of soothing the lions a bit, but much softer now because the Interloper might have made the connection and we don't want him turning up at this stage.

So far, so good. We have reached the end of phase one of the operation without any mishaps.

An hour later, we had the three lions laid out in a row behind the Land Rover. Petri had examined them all thoroughly and had given them each a tranquilliser, because Sernalyn is purely a muscle relaxant, and doesn't have any tranquillising effect.

Petri seemed very pleased with the way things had gone. 'Chris,' he remarked to me in his strong Afrikaans accent. 'I think everything is come out very well. We don't have any worries about the conditions of these lions. They reacted extremely well to the drug. I think, Chris, you were extremely good in finding them tonight, and we can all be very happy about the situation. It is time now to call up the support vehicles.'

We had some extra vehicles in the support party that night and had made one minor change in the transportation arrangements. Trish was there, driving Petri Viljoen's closed Toyota, and we had decided to load Vela on to that vehicle instead of the Volkswagen which was full of sightseers. There was another carload of spectators present which included the contractor who had planned and built the enclosure to which we were now going to take them.

The loading was hard work but everything went according to plan. We used nets in order to make the inert lions easier to handle, and we wore plastic gloves as arranged. I sat in the back of Keith's open Toyota with Charlotte, Tabs and Jack, with the two whites lying at our feet. Mike Dodds was perched with his camera on the tailboard of the Toyota, filming away, while Keith Joubert illuminated the scene for him with a sun gun. Frances Joubert was driving.

We drove very slowly, along paths that we had travelled so many, many times looking for these lions. Temba and Tombi seemed enormous stretched out in the truck; breathing deeply and looking sleek and well-fed and very, very white. Tombi had a slight scar on her shoulder, nothing serious, but when we were loading Vela on to Trish's vehicle we noticed that he had quite a bad wound on his back, probably a souvenir of an encounter with the Interloper. Well, at least they were safe from that hazard now.

When we arrived at Sing-Sing, we unloaded the lions very carefully and Petri took their temperatures, which were normal. Now there was nothing more to be done but leave them to recover from the effect of the drugs. We drove the vehicles out of the enclosure and locked the gates. It was 5.30 a.m.

Tryg went off in my jeep, playing the Beethoven at full blast, so there's yet another creature we've succeeded in getting hooked on Beethoven. So far the score, apart from myself, was three if not four lions, one hyena and one game warden. For the rest of my life I shall associate this music with the white lions and with this extraordinary episode. I couldn't really bring myself to believe it was now over.

After a fitful night's sleep, we went to Tryg's at about eleven o'clock in the morning to see how the lions were faring – Charlotte, Jack, Tabs and I. They were lolling around in the long grass, none too steady on their feet. Every few paces they would flop down, and they were making no effort to play. Obviously, the effect of the drugs had not quite worn off. It was like watching a slow-motion film of lions.

Suddenly Tabs coughed, and instinctively I rapped out a whispered command: 'Shut up!' Jack turned to me and remarked, very sadly, in Zulu, 'No need for shut up any more. The time for shut up is finished.'